Discovering HighScope-
A Teacher's Journal

Discovering HighScope— A Teacher's Journal

By Rebecca James

HIGHSCOPE
PRESS®

Ypsilanti, Michigan

Published by

HighScope® Press

A division of the
HighScope Educational Research Foundation
600 North River Street
Ypsilanti, Michigan 48198-2898
734.485.2000, FAX 734.485.0704

Orders: 800.40.PRESS; Fax: 800.442.4FAX; www.highscope.org
E-mail: *press@highscope.org*

Editor: Jennifer Burd
Proofreader: Katie Bruckner
Cover design, text design, production: Seling Design LLC
Photography:
Bob Foran — front cover (right), 2, 3, 4, 22, 32, 111, 118, 142, 161, 186, 189, 191, 195
Gregory Fox — front cover (left), xx (left), 6, 9, 14, 17, 19, 23, 25, 33, 43, 62, 73, 86,
    95, 113, 123, 136, 140, 150, 154, 165, 166, 175, 176, 187, 192, 196, 198, back cover
Lev Gartman — 207
Rebecca James — 30, 31, 34, 35, 36, 37, 41, 45, 46, 47, 53, 58, 59, 61, 67, 68, 70, 75, 77,
    80, 84, 88, 89, 102, 103, 109, 131, 133, 181 (middle), 183, 184
HighScope Staff — All other photos

Library of Congress Cataloging-in-Publication Data
James, Rebecca, 1983- author.
  Discovering HighScope : a teacher's journal / Rebecca James.
     pages cm
  Includes bibliographical references.
   ISBN 978-1-57379-677-4 (soft cover : alk. paper) 1. Education, Preschool--Michigan-
-Ypsilanti. 2. HighScope Demonstration Preschool (Ypsilanti, Mich.)--Curricula. 3. Ac-
tive learning--Michigan--Ypsilanti. I. Title.
   LB1140.245.Y67J36 2013
   372.2109774'35--dc23
                 2013002398

Printed in the United States of America
10 9 8 7 6 5 4 3 2 1

Dedication

For Grandma, whose interest in children, love for learning,
and passion for early childhood education continue
to inspire me every day. I love you.

Contents

Contents

Acknowledgments

I would like to thank the HighScope Early Childhood team, including Ann Epstein, Sue Gainsley, Linda Horne, Shannon Lockhart, Beth Marshall, Polly Neill, Kay Rush, Emily Thompson, and Mary Delcamp. Special thanks to Shannon for her daily mentorship and support throughout the entire teaching experience, to Sue for guiding me through my transition into the classroom, to Polly for her thorough and thoughtful review of this book, and to Beth for her guidance. I would also like to thank the entire editing team, including Joanne Tangorra, Katie Bruckner, Nancy Brickman, and especially my dedicated editor, Jennifer Burd. Appreciation also goes to Dr. Karen Paciorek, my early childhood professor and adviser at Eastern Michigan University, as well as to my former classmates and colleagues. Finally, a big "Thank you!" goes to the children, families, and community of the HighScope Demonstration Preschool and the greater HighScope Educational Research Foundation, as this book couldn't have been written without them. Finally, I extend warm thanks and love to Lev, to my parents and grandparents, and to all of my family and friends who have supported me. It has been a pleasure to work on this project.

— Becky James

Foreword

By Shannon Lockhart, HighScope Senior Early Childhood Specialist

The year chronicled in this book, when Becky James was hired to be one of the HighScope Demonstration Preschool teachers, was an unusual one for the preschool. As Becky arrived, we were in a transition after Sue Gainsley, who had been a strong teacher at the preschool for 13 years, moved into the preschool director's position. This meant bringing in a teacher who was brand new to the HighScope Curriculum with only three months of school left and the annual HighScope International Conference soon to take place, during which visitors would come to the Demonstration Preschool to watch the HighScope Curriculum in action. From Becky's point of view, this must have felt like "being fed to the wolves" because she had so much to learn in such a short period of time. This is not to say that we expected her to function like a seasoned HighScope teacher right off the bat, but we at least wanted her to know some of the basics of the curriculum so she could put them into action when other teachers came to observe at the preschool during conference week.

Sue mentored Becky for a week and a half when Becky arrived, after which time Becky and I were on our own as coteachers. Even though Becky came to us with experience teaching young children, I was impressed with how she jumped in with both feet and proved to be such a quick learner of the HighScope Curriculum. She even took the lead during discussions with visitors during the week of the international conference — a big responsibility. I had wanted to give her space to learn the curriculum and her own ways of doing things in the classroom; however, since the school year was coming to an end and certain tasks needed to be completed, it was pretty much on-the-spot training and on-the-spot learning. But we survived the year's end and felt we could begin the following year at a slower pace and with better preparation. I will go into more thoughts about the time I spent mentoring Becky, but first, a few reflections about when *I* began at HighScope.

Reflections on Being a New HighScope Teacher

I came to HighScope through a master's program that involved earning a degree from Oakland University and completing a field experience with HighScope. This put me directly into the classroom with two highly qualified HighScope consultants (Ruth Strubank and Ann Rogers), who were teaching at the time. As a newcomer to the HighScope Curriculum, I had many of the same thoughts and feelings that Becky had when she first came in (e.g., "Am I doing this right?" "What if this doesn't work?" "What if the children act out?" "How do I handle this situation?" "I am not as comfortable with this part of the day — will I have to lead?" "Well that just fell apart!" "Why didn't this didn't happen as I expected it to?" "I'm not getting this!" "Help!" and "Just get me through the day!").

Learning a New Curriculum

Learning a new curriculum is not easy. However, after working with the HighScope Curriculum for 20 years and training teachers to use the curriculum, I have found that one needs to be not only open to the curriculum but also *invested* in it — that is, to really absorb it and make it a part of oneself — to put it to its best use for teachers, children, and families. If one doesn't believe in the curriculum or tries to implement it haphazardly, then the curriculum will not work to its fullest, and issues will arise. This is true of any curriculum. A curriculum must be used and not left on a shelf somewhere, gathering dust or only picked up when activity ideas are needed.

In the way it is designed, the HighScope Curriculum actually forces you to look at it and use it. And even though I studied the curriculum in my undergraduate courses, it wasn't until I was held accountable with the children and other teachers that I started to truly understand the components of the daily routine, the subtlety and depth of adult-child interactions, and how active learning is integrated into all aspects of the preschool day.

To this day, both as a teacher and trainer, I constantly refer back to HighScope's Curriculum manuals when issues arise, when I have questions about whether I am doing something right, or when I need more depth to my understanding. And Becky had less than a month to absorb the basic curriculum components before the mass of visitors attending the HighScope International

Conference arrived on the scene! She did a wonderful job that spring, and she really grew as a teacher using the HighScope Curriculum throughout the next year.

Becky's Learning Journey

After her first few weeks at HighScope, during the summer, Becky was able to complete the HighScope Preschool Curriculum Course (PCC), which allowed her to view her two-and-a-half months' experience earlier in the year through the lens of the curriculum as a whole. This allowed her to begin the new school year better equipped. It was nice to start off the program year by walking Becky through the process of getting to know children and families through home visits. This allowed us to think about the materials presently in the classroom as well as those children enjoyed at home that we could add. We had several planning sessions prior to the beginning of school to arrange the classroom, to plan a parent information board, and to plan field trips and parent meetings that would take place throughout the year. But we spent most of our time discussing the children and assigning them to groups, which is never an easy task — especially if you have many newcomers.

When school began after Labor Day, I still wanted to give Becky space to come into her own style of teaching while using the HighScope Curriculum. So I mentored her through modeling, through our morning prep discussions, and — most important — through our daily planning sessions.

Encouragement Versus Praise

As noted earlier, Becky was a quick study, and the curriculum knowledge she gained from the summer training she took also made a difference in her work in the classroom and in our daily planning process. For example, one-and-a-half months after she began teaching, we realized we needed to discuss the strategy of using encouragement instead of praise. All teachers, including me, have used praise before fully understanding the negative effects of words like "Good job," "That's beautiful," or "I like the way you…." It was a delicate issue to bring up because we didn't want to offend Becky; however, because of what we know about young children and what is best for them, Sue Gainsley and I talked to Becky about commenting descriptively to children about what they are doing rather than saying something to the children like "Good Job" or making judgments about children's work with words such as "I like." In addition, Becky learned about this issue from HighScope's *Moving Past*

Praise DVD and some articles on praise. Later that summer she attended the PCC and learned more about all of HighScope's adult-child interaction strategies. Through these initial teaching experiences and her summer studies, I felt Becky really got this strategy down — by the time we started off the new school year, encouragement was one of her strengths.

Transitions

In our preschool routine, recall time is followed by washing hands and snacktime. When school began again in the fall, the transitions from cleanup to recall to washing hands and then to snack seemed to be the most difficult times of the day for both Becky and the children. Becky and I spent many planning sessions addressing strategies for handling these times. She noticed that children were not settling down for recall, nor were they listening to each other at recall time. We talked about having her use more concrete recall strategies as well as strategies in which children hold something in their hands to keep them engaged, which Becky describes in more detail later on in this book. (This helps children feel less like they are waiting for a turn and, instead, being more engaged with each other.) We also discussed how Becky could talk with the children about being respectful when someone else is talking. In addition, Becky talked with a couple children about sitting by each other, which they really wanted to do, and how they needed to listen to each other's recalls. I let Becky know that it was okay for her to talk to children when she was frustrated and to discuss with them how to solve the issue together. Throughout the year, I watched Becky grow a great deal in the areas of transitions and problem solving.

Becky said she observed that children tended to wander after washing their hands — which would lengthen snacktime because jobs were not getting done or there was a conflict over who was going to sit in the favorite middle seat at our table that has a cutaway. Some children would linger in the bathroom or wander the room after washing their hands, and Becky describes in this book the strategies that we discussed to help children have a transition that offered more opportunities for active learning. This transition is all about having fun and having choices, even when a task has to be done.

Conflict Resolution

One other aspect of the curriculum that challenged Becky, as it does all teachers, was implementation of the six conflict resolution steps. Although this aspect of adult-child interaction started off slow for Becky, in the end she became a real pro! She initially seemed pretty comfortable with the process, but as different conflicts arose, the steps didn't always work as she had hoped they would. Like any new strategy, practicing these steps takes lots of practice. Even as a seasoned teacher, I am still learning to use this process with children, including how to decide what to do when there are different temperaments involved. But I also know that acknowledging children's feelings is the most powerful thing we can do, and that, if I don't keep this step in mind for the whole process, it can make or break the end result (including the length of a conflict situation).

When Becky and I would talk after school about the conflicts that occurred that day, it led us to thinking about the six steps. Doing so reminded me that at times I needed to write into our daily plan that we should be sure to acknowledge children's feelings, because it had felt to me as though we hadn't been using that step as much. We found that focusing on this really helped with the children whose emotions would get the best of them. We had noticed that, if their feelings were not acknowledged, then their emotions intensified, and the problem-solving process took longer or even that the issue popped up again at a later time.

Another part of Becky's problem-solving learning process that I was able to offer help with was asking for children's ideas. Soon after Becky started teaching, I noticed that when children couldn't come up with ideas for solving problems, she sometimes would offer a closed-ended idea, such as putting the item in dispute away. Sometimes the children's issue would then come up again later because it was not completely resolved for them.

During our daily planning time, Becky and I talked about how we want children to come up with the solutions themselves — whether their solution makes sense to us or not — and that we need to continue to explore solutions until the children agree on a plan. This can feel difficult if it is taking a long time and no one is coming up with ideas. But we know it is important to stick with the process until all sides have agreed on the outcome. I let Becky know that our process always involves taking it back to the children and saying "We haven't come up with an agreement yet" or "Your idea is not going to work for her so we have to come up with another idea" or "We haven't solved the problem yet, so what do you think we can do to solve this problem?" That is, I ask questions and making comments until I feel the children have really tried to come up with ideas. If they are still stuck, and I think the problem solving is not going anywhere or is collapsing back into intense emotions, then I generally ask if they would like to hear my idea. However, I think too many times we don't give children enough time before we chime in with our own ideas, because we want the problem to end quickly. But if we pause and keep acknowledging feelings and asking for solutions, children *will* come up with ideas.

Strengths Becky Brought to the Preschool

Working with Becky was a wonderful experience. Her fresh ideas about children's needs and interests, about teaching children, and about planning for children were very much welcomed and made our year of teaching together engaging and rewarding. A highlight this year was how we made great connections with the children's parents, and I think it was Becky's e-mails to parents that started the whole process. Parents also began communicating with one other through e-mail, and even started getting together after preschool for play dates and extracurricular field trips. Of course, we would communicate in person with parents during morning dropoff and afternoon pickup times to share what had happened during the day, new things we'd observed about children's development, and any problems that had arisen. But our conversations with parents seemed more in-depth this year, and I think that the way Becky was proactive about using e-mail with parents contributed to that. We also had good turnouts for family potlucks and even for some parent meetings. This had also been true in the past, but this year the relationships seemed more open, and this was all enhanced by Becky's continued connections with parents and other family members.

Becky also has another strength that she probably doesn't even realize — her initiative. As an early childhood specialist at HighScope, I had many responsibilities outside of teaching in our half-day preschool classroom. At times these took me away to facilitate training sessions. Additionally, when I was in the office, I often just didn't have the time to dedicate to things like arranging field trips, labeling, printing pictures for the classroom, or making photo books. Becky took all of these tasks upon herself. She became the "label queen," as I kept telling her! Sometimes during planning, we would be talking about some good ideas, and the next thing I'd know, she'd be carrying them out. As a new teacher she showed great initiative, and I knew that I could depend on her.

Although Becky had developed many skills for working with young children before she came to HighScope, she also worked hard at learning the curriculum and the adult-child interaction strategies that do not come as naturally. She studied the way I did when I first came — she read through the HighScope Curriculum books, she watched HighScope DVDs, and she was thoroughly engaged in the HighScope trainings she took — which allowed her to internalize her understandings and put the curriculum into action in the classroom.

Mentoring Becky, Learning From Becky

As I think back on mentoring Becky, and what would be helpful for new teachers and mentors, I think daily planning is probably the most powerful teaching and mentoring agent in this whole process. In these daily sessions, Becky and I had the opportunity to discuss how the day went; talk about our strengths and our weaknesses; and bounce new ideas off one another. We solved problems and took a look at children's development in depth and sometimes just talked about how we could be more true to ourselves as teachers. Becky picked up on strategies from me and I, from her.

Even as a seasoned teacher, I still look to the HighScope Curriculum to help me in the classroom, just as Becky did. Besides *The HighScope Preschool Curriculum* book set, I recommend using the resources that the curriculum provides (the website at www.highscope.org, online video clips, online small- and large-group-time ideas from teachers, curriculum DVDs, teacher idea books, content books, online training, and face-to-face training). These are all tools to help us better understand the curriculum and young children, and to make us more intentional as teachers. Additionally, the HighScope Demonstration Preschool, which hosts visitors from all over the world, is a great place to observe and learn.

A final recommendation for anyone who wants to learn about the curriculum is to ask questions of your mentor and to lean on your mentor — especially when things aren't working the way you had expected them to. Reflect together on each day and each part of the day until they are making sense for you and the children. Just as we ask children to reflect on their work time, we need to reflect on our teaching so that we can create a positive, active learning environment, implement a daily routine that meets the needs of the children and the teachers, and become more supportive, responsive teachers who are intentional in our interactions and our plans to facilitate optimal learning. It can be done. Becky James's experience proves that this is absolutely true!

In the remainder of this book you will follow Becky's HighScope learning journey as she tells it in her own words. First, in Chapter 1, you will read her reflections on various parts of the HighScope Curriculum after her first six weeks at the Demonstration Preschool, when she was filling an absence at the end of the school year. In Chapter 2, Becky describes going on home visits and getting the classroom ready for the upcoming school year. The subsequent chapters then describe, month by month (September through June), Becky's classroom experiences during a full program year, and what she learned from them.

The book also includes two appendixes. In Appendix A you will find the HighScope Preschool Curriculum Content — key developmental indicators organized under eight content areas. In Appendix B, you will find some suggested resources in particular areas that Becky has reflected on in her journals.

— Shannon Lockhart

(*Editor's Note:* The names of the children the author mentions in this book have been changed to protect the privacy of the children and their families.)

As a HighScope teaching team, Becky and Shannon practice intentional planning and have fun too!

Chapter 1

Getting to Know HighScope

I joined the HighScope Demonstration Preschool at the end of March, after a challenging year of teaching in South America. The Demonstration Preschool children and staff had also been through numerous changes in the previous months. Shannon Lockhart had been the only consistent teacher throughout the year, and now that I was on board, the children in my small group were working with their third teacher of the year. (Our classroom is staffed with two teachers, each of whom takes responsibility for half the group at small-group times.) In addition to these changes in the teachers, a student had recently moved away, leaving an opening that was filled by a new child.

Thoughts on My First Six Weeks

With the exception of some basic information discussed in my early childhood education graduate courses, HighScope was new to me when I started teaching at the Demonstration Preschool. Although I'd had some teaching experience with toddlers and preschoolers, and had held various positions in kindergarten through grade five classrooms, I'd had no formal HighScope training or even much time to begin reading about the program before jumping into the classroom. Thankfully, Sue Gainsley (the teacher transitioning out of the classroom) was able to stay for more than a week, and this made the transition easier for all of us. Sue's new position as full-time Early Childhood

During planning time, I talk with a child about her work-time plans.

Specialist included serving as my mentor. Then, after only a week and a half, spring break fell, so I was able to attend the "Daily Routine" portion of the Preschool Curriculum Course (PCC). The timing of this training was perfect for me, coming as it did after I'd had the opportunity to get a feel for the classroom and program and to consult with colleagues and other resources. My training continues, but here are my reflections on some components of the HighScope Curriculum that surprised me during my first six weeks at the Demonstration Preschool.

Shared control

When I first started in the HighScope classroom, I had difficulty drawing the line between children doing whatever they wanted and my ideas on how to keep experiences safe and appropriate. I had never felt this sort of confusion before. I usually am able to instinctively form and follow a decision regarding classroom management or other practices. Because I didn't have all of the information when I first started at HighScope, I had only a vague understanding of the way children and adults share control in HighScope classrooms. In fact, the concept of *shared control* really struck a chord with me during my training at HighScope. Prior to that, I hadn't come across the concept of shared control in either my HighScope preparation or in my previous early childhood education courses. Throughout this book, I refer to various elements of shared control, especially as I question my thinking (asking myself "Why not?").

I've begun to question some of the more traditional rules I've come to follow and expect of my students. For example, one day during my first week in the HighScope classroom, Veronica became upset because she wasn't finished with her small-group experience, but everyone was getting ready for outside time. I wasn't sure yet what the "rules" were about outside time. I assumed that the small-group materials shouldn't be taken outside, so I acknowledged Veronica's feelings and asked her if she would like to

A work-in-progress sign communicates that the child who built this sculpture intends to do more work on it at a later time.

I observe attentively and acknowledge a child's work with beads.

use a "Work in Progress" sign (a sign with a circle and slash over a graphic of a hand to indicate that the work-in-progress should not be touched) on her work. When Sue then suggested that Veronica could finish outside, I thought, "But of course!" I hadn't known this was an option but thought, Why wouldn't it be?

I've since become accustomed to questioning many of my initial reactions in the same way. I had been habitually stopping to consider what the rules might be for a given situation, but now I also consider whether a rule I've learned somewhere along the way in my career might actually compromise a learning opportunity. My goal is always to be mindful of what is in the best interests of children. Now I have a working understanding of the balance between adult and child decisions in the classroom. That doesn't mean I can't set limits but, rather, that I shouldn't impose a restriction simply because I am accustomed to doing so. I want my decisions to be purposeful.

Praise versus encouragement

When I arrived at HighScope, I had no idea that using praising language was even an early childhood issue. I often used phrases like "Kyra, I like the way that you helped Norah with the paint." While I wasn't constantly making blanket "Good Job!" statements, the idea that praise enhances children's self-esteem was embedded in my brain. After my HighScope training, I learned to respond to children's accomplishments a little differently. For example, I would now speak to Kyra like this: "Kyra, you helped Norah with the paint. Now the two of you can paint together." What's more, I didn't even realize that eliminating praise in the classroom was considered an effective early childhood practice! I had never heard about it, much less read of studies sharing the drawbacks of praise. Thankfully, I had a mentor in Sue, who helped break it to me gently that HighScope meaningfully encourages and acknowledges children rather than praising their efforts. Since then I have turned to HighScope resources, including the *Extensions* curriculum newsletter and the *Moving Past Praise* DVD, as well as learning from my colleagues and training sessions.

Problem solving

In some ways, from the very beginning I was quite comfortable with the way that HighScope handles problem solving in social conflict situations. I'd had experience using similar approaches with young children in early childhood and early elementary settings. Approaching calmly and acknowledging children's feelings, the first two steps in HighScope's problem-solving process, were both important steps in the approaches I had applied in the past. It felt natural for me to discuss the problem with children, isolating an object in question if necessary, and arriving at a possible solution

The Six Steps to Conflict Resolution

1. Approach calmly, stopping any hurtful actions.
2. Acknowledge children's feelings.
3. Gather information.
4. Restate the problem.
5. Ask for ideas for solutions and choose one together.
6. Give follow-up support as needed.

together. However, I realized that, in my past experience, there were three key elements to this process that I had overlooked at times.

The first key element relates to sharing my own ideas for solutions. In HighScope's approach, we ask children having a conflict to suggest ways to solve the problem. In these situations, of course, I will usually have some ideas of my own about what might work. Although I try to allow the children to generate possible solutions without my expressed input, sometimes it can be helpful to share my thoughts as a last resort. My coteachers have modeled this language: "Would you like to hear my idea?"

The second key element I've discovered has been remembering to follow up and re-acknowledge feelings when needed. Sometimes the steps need to be repeated, and going back to acknowledging feelings seemed so basic that I had often overlooked this. The third key element involves staying with the children until the problem is resolved (*really* resolved). This is something that I didn't fully understand until after my first few weeks at the Demonstration

I work with children on resolving a conflict.

Preschool. Sometimes a problem will arise and children have difficulty sticking with the mutually agreed-upon solution.

I remember when the idea of staying with the children until the very end really struck me: It was during greeting time on a day much like any other in the classroom. Shannon was greeting parents at the door, and I was reading books to children on the carpet. DeShawn was intent on reading the new book, a photo album of our field trip to a pizza restaurant. Although he was finished with the photo album, and it was just sitting in his lap as he read a different book altogether, he did not want anyone else to have a turn with the album. I had already talked to him about it, and to be honest, I remember feeling not completely confident about how to handle it. These were the first few weeks, and I was still developing my ideas about shared control, as I mentioned. I approached DeShawn, acknowledged that he was excited about the new book, but also rephrased what another child had said — that he wanted to use the book too. After restating the problem, I asked the boys for ideas. The second child, Clyde, thought that they could both look at the book together, but DeShawn didn't want anything to do with that. So I stated my idea — that perhaps, if DeShawn didn't want to read it together with Clyde, when DeShawn was finished he could give it to Clyde for a turn.

Turn taking. DeShawn and Clyde's story brings up something else I've learned — that children do not readily grasp the idea of taking turns. Although I know this, adults often use the phrase "take turns" without trying to understand what it might mean from the child's perspective. For example, some children will say, "You can take turns" when we're trying to solve a problem with them. Shannon and I will then say, "What does that mean?" And the kids will eventually say something like "He can have it first and then after the sand timer is done, I can have it" or "I can use it today and he can use it tomorrow." These are two very different interpretations of taking turns.

Whether children are using these terms in response to adult prompting or on their own (as sometimes happens, particularly if *take turns* is a phrase often used at home), it's always important to find out what the child means. For example, when I ask a child what he means after proposing turn-taking as a solution, as Clyde sometimes does, he might say, "DeShawn can read the book, and when he's done, it's my turn to have it." If I press him further by asking how he'll know when DeShawn is finished, he may say, "Get the sand timer." Then I have to ask DeShawn if he is okay with that solution. And he might not be. Sometimes it can seem like a child says no just to say no.

We all have children who struggle with problem solving, and some days are harder than others. I remember struggling to work with DeShawn and Clyde, trying out various strategies with them, and then turning my attention back to another student who also needed me. I didn't stick with the problem. Shannon then came over and went back through the six steps to conflict resolution with DeShawn and Clyde, as well as with another child who now also wanted a turn with the book. I don't remember the exact words that Shannon used that day. She did, however, teach me that I need to stick with problem solving until it is resolved. This doesn't mean that the same problem won't occur again, but at least the children involved will have an understanding that they resolved the problem together, that their voices were heard, and that their feelings and opinions matter. This particular situation made a light bulb go off in my head. *Stay until the problem is solved.*

Talking to my coteacher. I also learned to lean on my teaching partner. Conflicts and disputes between children frequently happened during greeting time, and while I would be working with children on those, other issues would also often come up, requiring my attention. Now I know that I can call my coteacher over to take care of any new issue that comes up so that I can stay with the original one. And the children *will* come to a solution. They *will* figure it out. Sometimes they will come up with new ideas, or they may repeat ideas that have or have not been successful in the past. They may even refuse to problem-solve until they give up and move on to something else; but eventually you will get there with them.

One more piece of the problem-solving puzzle fell into place for me when I realized that it also helps to invite other children to help solve a different kind of problem. The classroom is a true community, and children are interested in what is happening around them. It's so much more obvious to me that it helps to call on the ideas of other children when solving problems with materials, for example. That is, if a child is struggling with the tape, I might say, "Earlier I saw Mina trying to get some tape too. She tried something different when she couldn't get it to work. You could ask Mina how she did that." This can also work when it comes to resolving social conflicts. The children learn together and from one another. It's often been helpful for me to rely on the ideas of children who are not directly involved in a problem situation. Some of these children are more experienced problem-solvers and some just have a different perspective. Further, problem solving just seems to come more naturally to some children than it does to others. Moreover, children who struggle to problem-solve may feel more confident in their abilities when approached to help another child with a problem that they are not so emotionally connected to.

Social stories. Social stories are another helpful strategy for both individual and cooperative problem-solving situations. When I first began at HighScope, I understood the value of and loved the concept of using a personalized literacy experience (incorporating writing, reading, and shared language) to help children solve problems.

One of the first times that I really felt the power of the social story was when we worked through an impromptu hair-cutting issue. That day, DeShawn

Children look on as I listen to Miriam explain why she wanted the paint to go on the table. Another child had suggested that it was a problem. One child thought it was okay as long as she cleaned up when she was finished. Together the group came to a solution. With acknowledgment of Miriam's feelings and suggestions from others, all decide that it's okay to get paint on the table, but that, next time, Miriam could use the art area so other children could use this house-area table for a party — and of course, the art area is equipped with tile floor and a sink for easy clean up.

was experimenting with a scissors in the block area. Before we knew it, De-Shawn cut a small chunk out of Declan's hair, and Declan wasn't very happy. Avery had been watching closely, and he had a scissors in his hand too. The whole situation seemed important enough not only to problem solve on the spot but also to bring it up again with a message on the message board the next day. So I started a social story with a simple stick drawings, including a child with a scissors and a sad child with a chunk of hair missing. This was my first solo attempt to use this strategy, and it was a great first experience for me.

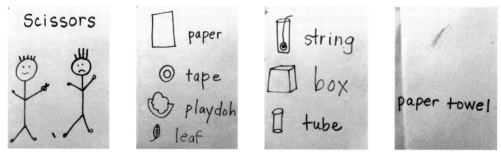

This social story shows the children's ideas — after one child cut another child's hair — about what is appropriate for children to cut with scissors. Later, Declan added another material to the story that could be cut — a paper towel.

The story unfolded during message board time the next day as a simple list of things that were okay to use with scissors — which was much like the beginning of a conversation I'd had with the involved children the previous day. After looking at the stick-figure drawings from the social story I'd created and had taped to the message board, the whole group came up with ideas about what we could cut with scissors: paper, tape, play dough, fallen leaves, string, cardboard boxes or tubes, and so forth. I listed each item on paper as the children mentioned them, using both words and pictures, and we completed the social story book together as a class. Declan arrived late, and when I read the book to him, he added the idea that we could cut paper towels with scissors. I wrote the words *paper towel* on one of the pages in the book, and he drew the picture. Now we have the *Scissors* social story on our class bookshelf, and the kids read through it during greeting time, snacktime, or work time.

Planning and recall

Planning and recall are one aspect of the HighScope Curriculum that I had learned about through some of my early childhood courses, but that didn't mean I knew how to implement them in the classroom! I was fully behind the idea of doing so since I understood the importance of planning and recall, but I was somewhat hesitant in my approach to planning for these experiences. Little did I know that planning and recall times could be so simple. It was hard for me to expand my mindset and come up with new ways to do planning and recall when I didn't have a fully developed idea of how these experiences played out for children. When I realized that materials could provide a catalyst for conversation, I started to have a better idea of what I could use as planning and recall strategies.

I remember when Shannon (my coteacher) used Duplo blocks with area signs for planning because a number of the children in her group had been using these blocks during work time. Her strategy was to give the children Duplo people figures and have the child put the Duplo figure on the block next to the area sign where the child wanted to play. This was something of an epiphany for me. It sounds so silly, but when I realized that I could begin by using a material based on the children's interests, planning and recall became less about "Oh my gosh, am I doing this right?!" and more about finding what worked best for my group, reflecting on key developmental indicators (KDIs) or Child Observation Record (COR) items I had observed or wanted to encourage, using a variety of concrete and abstract activities, and simply experiencing planning and recall language with the children. (For more on the KDIs and the COR, see "KDIs and the COR" on p. 12. You will also find a complete list of the HighScope curriculum content areas and KDIs in Appendix A.) There are so many great planning and recall strategies that already work well, but I love the chance to be creative and come up with new ideas as well — not only ideas that take into account the children's interests but also ones that suit my group's developmental levels.

After I started to visualize planning and recall strategies that would work, I also realized that many strategies could be used for both planning and recall times. For example, children can look through a tube to find the material or area they plan to use/go to, as well as to recall which materials they used or where they went to play. However, there are some strategies that just work better for planning and some that just work better for recall. For example, the idea of Duplo constructions lends itself to planning because I have more time to set it up before work time. Also, the children have more time to become invested in writing during recall time, so something like making a recall book or writing what they did works better for recall time.

Important Notes

KDIs and the COR

I have found the key developmental indicators (KDIs) and the Child Observation Record (COR) to be enormously helpful in understanding children's development.

Key Developmental Indicators (KDIs)

KDIs are the building blocks of thinking, reasoning, and learning at each stage of development. The KDIs can be found everywhere in what children say and do. After learning about the KDIs, I was able to understand what children were learning and experiencing and could help them build on that. Or if I noticed that they weren't engaging in certain KDIs, I could develop an activity or suggest some materials that would help them grow in that area.

The KDIs are organized into the following eight content areas: Approaches to Learning; Social and Emotional Development; Physical Development and Health; Language, Literacy, and Communication; Mathematics; Creative Arts; Science and Technology; and Social Studies. You can find a complete list of content areas and KDIs in Appendix A, on pages 201–203.

Child Observation Record (COR)

The Child Observation Record (COR) is a comprehensive assessment tool that evaluates children's learning across content areas. Using the COR, teachers observe children, write up their observations in daily anecdotes that objectively describe children's behavior, and use these anecdotal notes to assess children's learning and development. This process also helps teachers plan activities to help children develop in particular areas.

The COR was one of the first tools that I became familiar with when beginning my work at HighScope. I was overwhelmed by the prospect of learning this assessment method, but I was also excited. I found it helpful to think about where my new children were developmentally, as well as to look ahead at what I might expect of them (each of them differently) in the coming months. Working through anecdotes, reading anecdotal samples, and understanding how to write objective notes were all part of this process as I grew more comfortable with the COR.

Likewise, there are some strategies that don't work as well for Shannon's group as they do for mine, and vice versa. It just depends on the children's developmental levels and interests. For example, I love the idea of planning under the table; but with my current group, this just tends to get too silly, which takes away from the planning experience. On the other hand, my group loves to use the Hula Hoop. We sing in a circle on the floor while spinning the Hula Hoop between all of our hands, and when the song ends, the child whose hand is touching the taped part of the hoop does the planning or recall. However, this strategy doesn't work as well with the other group. Sometimes the children argue over who ends up with the tape, so sometimes we might choose not to use the Hula Hoop as a planning or recall strategy, though other times we'll work through it as a problem solving opportunity.

Large-group time

I have to ask myself, why has this been such a mental struggle for me? As I am a singer, large-group time is one of the parts of the day that I love most in the early childhood classroom. I have always loved the part of the daily routine that includes movement and music activities — often called "circle time," "get-together time," or "time to exercise our brains." I'm fascinated with how children become engaged in the stories, rhymes, movements, and songs put to music or simple rhythms. Nevertheless, I hit some road blocks with this part of the daily routine when I first came to HighScope. Part of it was that I didn't know some of the songs the teachers and children sang, or I was familiar with a different version. And I didn't even really know what materials we had for use at large-group time. However, the greater challenges stemmed from being a large-group-time beginner. That is, I didn't understand how to best incorporate choice during large-group time. I've been comfortable with the children making choices about how to move their bodies, for example, but it has taken a while for me to more naturally acknowledge children's movement ideas, such as how they dance or move with a scarf, for example. Once again, I had to rethink my approach.

I've learned several things along the way. For example, in a key developmental indicators (KDIs) workshop I went to during the HighScope International Conference in May, I first heard about the idea of separation when teaching movement to children: that is, to either do the movement without describing it OR to describe the movement without doing it. For example, if my intention is for the children to tap their head, I could choose to show this simply by doing, perhaps introducing it by saying, "Watch and copy."

At first I didn't even know how to distinguish an easy-to-join activity from other large-group activities. I also didn't understand the reason behind this activity: that it helps create a fluid transition from the previous part of the day to the main large-group activity. In addition, I thought we needed to keep the kids only in the carpet area (where we typically hold large-group time). This illustrates one instance (of many) where I have learned to ask myself *why* I needed to be rigid about this boundary. Yes, there are many situations in which we do stay on the carpet because of the lack of space in other parts of the classroom for gross-motor movements. But this doesn't mean that we can't think of ways to move about the room creatively or go beyond the rug area as long as the children have room to jump, twirl, or move about in the ways they choose.

Early on, I learned that we do not use music recordings with words at the Demonstration Preschool. I was surprised to think that this was even an issue, but I knew that the ideas behind our HighScope practices are based on

Adults try out children's ideas with them at large-group time.

important research in the field of early childhood education. When it was explained to me that music on typical children's albums can be too fast and also leave little room for the children's ideas, I heard the explanation, but it wasn't until I'd had enough experience with large-group time at the Demonstration Preschool that I really understood it.

I have also learned that the children can have a strong voice in how large-group time is carried out. Each child has multiple opportunities to interpret and share how an activity sounds, looks, and feels. Once I truly absorbed this idea, I realized that many of my past large-group times, as fun or well-meaning as they had been, probably just grazed the surface of the participant ownership that allows children to make large-group time a most authentic experience. Thankfully, as it happens, it's really not that difficult to take some of those favorite songs and think of ways to adapt them so the children can take the lead. Children have even surprised me by thinking of ways to change songs that I hadn't considered!

Small-group time

As I have mentioned, I have felt very supported by my coteachers, as well as by the whole team of educators with which I am most fortunate to work. However, I have still experienced some anxiety as an adjusting teacher, and although the close of a school day would celebrate another day of survival in the classroom, it also meant that our daily planning would soon commence. Since my first preschool experience in another childcare setting, I haven't quite felt as though I excel in planning for preschoolers. So, in the early months, I struggled to think of small-group ideas, mainly because I was still developing an understanding about what small-group time really was. There were times early on when I felt like I needed to come up with a great plan on the spot.

I really leaned on my coteachers and mentors at the beginning, and talking with them taught me first to thoughtfully consider students' interests. In the beginning, it helped me to think of a particular material of interest first and then decide how to narrow the focus of the small-group plan to a KDI or COR item that would illustrate the children's development in a particular area. Later I learned that small-group time is a great way to introduce the children to new experiences or types of experiences that they may have overlooked during work time. For example, a child who often plans to work in the block area or at the sand and water table may still continue to engage in experiences there but may bring over materials he or she has newly discovered that are typically be found in the toy or house areas.

Along the way I also came to understand that small-group opening statements can be easier to develop than I had thought. I had always put thought into these introductions, of course; but I began to understand that simplicity once again is the key in small-group time planning. After one week of HighScope PCC training that focused on the daily routine, I learned just how simply we can set the stage for our learners. We can shift the focus to content areas or children's interests, or we can open with a short story or basic description of the materials. Knowing that I have these four options, and remembering that there's no set way to go about it, has made this a more creative and positive process.

Initially, I was not even aware of HighScope's math and literacy programs. Once I had begun to acquire a feel for the daily routine, daily planning with my teaching partner, and supportive adult-child interactions, I was able to look through some of HighScope's Teacher Idea Books and the Numbers Plus and Growing Readers curriculum kits, as well as other curriculum materials, and get an even broader picture of the HighScope Curriculum. I briefly paged through the books and other resources with the sole intention of pulling in little hints and tidbits that would help me understand the bigger picture. When I had a hard time planning for small-group time, I looked to Numbers Plus or Growing Readers for some ideas. My coteacher, Shannon, and mentor, Sue, would also refer me to some of their favorites during planning time, and I'd choose an activity that I thought would interest the children or help me to observe more of the KDIs or COR items in context.

The first activity that I chose from Numbers Plus was a number sense activity called "Cake Cutting." The children in my group had been very interested in using play dough as well as hosting very elaborate birthday parties during work time. I adjusted the activity to fit the needs of my students of course, but this idea card from the Numbers Plus box was a springboard, and I especially found it helpful for supporting children at various developmental levels. The scaffolding ideas included on the Numbers Plus cards helped me to see how the developmental range could be worded on our daily planning sheets for any learning experience.

I kept the activity simple. The idea was to expose the children to the notion of composing and decomposing — make a cake and then cut it into pieces. In the end, the children were more interested in the "candles" (Cuise-

Shannon gets down at children's level and talks with the children about what they are doing at small-group time.

naire rods that I had set aside as a backup material) than in cutting pieces of cake for people at the party. The children used the materials in ways that interested them and that gave them various experiences with math concepts, such as counting. It ended up being a lot like the "Counting Candles" and "Birthday Cake" activities, so I was also able to look at those cards and plan variations on those small-group experiences.

Daily planning and scaffolding

At the end of each day, Shannon and I share our thoughts and ideas with one another and plan activities and interactions for the next day. As a team, we openly discuss how particular strategies worked, what we found challenging, what things went well, what we might try next time, and any other parts of our day that we want to make sure we are both aware of. As a teacher new to HighScope, this part of my day — paired with the classroom experience — was the best training I could ever get. In fact, most of the ideas discussed throughout this introduction were first reflected on informally with Shannon during our daily planning.

Planning with a purpose is one of the most important concepts that I have begun to fine-tune through my HighScope experiences. Although I have always had the best of intentions for purposeful planning, I realized that there are elements of the day that I hadn't given a spare thought to. When Shannon and I plan, we follow a consistent format based on the daily routine. We plan "lessons" of course (large- and small-group times, for example), but we also plan what we will discuss with the children when we meet in the morning (using the message board), how we anticipate the children will use materials, how we anticipate children will describe materials and actions (including how we will scaffold children's learning as they do so), what we will do for transitions between parts of the daily routine, and what materials we will have outdoors during outside time.

These are all very important things to consider when planning for the children's day. Of course, we keep a sense of flexibility, but we are also very intentional. For example, we think ahead about the *best* way to transition and the strategies that we think will work for cleanup time at a particular point in the year. I didn't usually plan messages ahead of time in my elementary classroom experiences. I didn't plan the transitions, either. I've learned that by planning these small but important moments, I become more conscious of my students' needs, strengths, and interests.

"Make a conscious effort to write anecdotes that will not only help with COR assessing, but to share student interests for planning, recall, and small-group planning." This is a note that I wrote to myself during my first week of training. I had been consistently taking anecdotes, but I learned that simply jotting down some examples of things children are interested in and things not necessarily tied to a specific COR item (for the purpose of recording an anecdote later) helped to jog my memory during that afternoon's planning. It was as simple as writing down the phrase "Pegboards: Sophie and Veronica" so that I would remember those two children choosing that material during a particularly engaged work time. Perhaps I could incorporate that material into planning or small group, I thought. I could also remind Shannon of that, too, since one of the girls is in her group.

Identifying what students may do in earlier, middle, or later stages of development helps me as the teacher to think ahead about how I might scaf-

Shannon and I discuss anecdotes, observations, and challenges as we plan for the next day.

fold children's learning at small-group time — that is, how I can support and extend the children's various approaches to small-group experiences. Although — as with many elements of my training — this was somewhat difficult to grasp at first, my growing understanding of this concept became so helpful in terms of aligning purpose with development. Thinking about small-group time in this way helped me get to know my students after arriving late in the school year. Still, putting the earlier, middle, and later stages into words is a great challenge. And I especially had difficulty with this when visitors (people who come to HighScope to observe the Demonstration Preschool in action via closed-circuit television) were watching me plan! However, this is a team ef-fort, and we work to support one another. Shannon has helped me understand that naming the COR items or KDIs that will be part of the activity's focus — before forming my ideas for earlier-middle-later — is key to maintaining the purpose behind the plan.

COR items and KDIs

I had some confusion early on about the difference between the COR items and the KDIs. (For more on COR items and KDIs, see p. 12. In Appendix A you will also find a complete list of curriculum content areas and KDIs.) Actually, I had unknowingly paid little attention to the KDIs because I was focused on matching the COR items with anecdotes. I'd had some experience with taking anecdotes, but I had a hard time matching each interesting comment or instance of reasoning with a specific COR item, whether or not I had a KDI in mind instead. I found it difficult to avoid stretching an item to make it fit something else, especially when anecdotes illustrated a child's sense of reason.

I had to rely on Shannon and Sue for some clarification with this. Going through some of the students' past anecdotes and reading sample anecdotes really helped as well. (The OnlineCOR has sample anecdotes that I have found extremely helpful.) Not only was I able to gauge where my students were, developmentally, but I also learned how to group anecdotes under the correct COR items. In doing so, I also realized that I had been omitting some very important COR items unintentionally. That is, while I engaged in experiences with children and observed their explorations, I tended to write up anecdotes that cited items in the areas of social relations, creative representation, and mathematics and science. I realized that language and literacy, particularly using vocabulary and patterns of speech, was something that I had been taking for granted. After realizing this and discussing it with Shannon, we intentionally planned to focus on taking anecdotes primarily related to language and literacy. We wrote it directly into the work-time section of our planning sheet — a practice that is a great way to remind ourselves what our personal teaching goals are for the day or week.

Looking back, I realized that I didn't think to write anecdotes during outside time throughout my first few weeks. Eventually, I caught some really great snapshots of active learning at outside time through such notes, which were just as valid, if not more vivid, than my notes taken during indoor experiences. I've also learned that writing whole-group anecdotes is a good strategy when observing the children developing skills during a large- or small-group experience. For example, I jotted down the names of five children who were keeping a steady beat during our easy-to-join activity at large-group time one morning, and I later transferred this information to the COR.

Materials

The words "I wonder what you might do with these" have completely opened up the creative possibilities of small-group time for me. I've learned that we can use just about any material in the classroom — purchased, recycled, found, natural, or homemade — including materials as classic as wooden blocks, as exciting as Bubber (a modeling compound), or as simple as dirt. I wrote another note to myself in one of my early training packets: "Remember that small-group time can be simpler than you usually think."

I remember one day in May, when my HighScope colleague Polly Neill subbed in the classroom. She was hoping to engage the children in a creative representation activity for small-group time. She planned to use Legos and people and animal figures to allow for storytelling through making models and pretending. What I found especially interesting was that Polly also chose to use stones. She envisioned the children perhaps using the stones as a fence or a barrier for the animals. In the end, the children focused on the Legos and did a great deal of construction without using many stones or animals, but that didn't matter. I remember this as a way to think about using any materials in as many ways as possible. For instance, stones aren't just for pretending to cook, for one-to-one correspondence, or for play in the sand and water table. All of these materials have open-ended possibilities!

Choosing materials and trying to gauge where children who are at various developmental levels will take their experiences does not have to mean I *know* where the experience will go. This is the beauty of the open-ended experience. I really mean it when I say to the children, "I wonder what you might do with these materials" — a statement born of true curiosity!

To give another example, I said the same thing to the children when I gave them different sized boxes along with scissors and tape (as a backup material). I thought they might stack the boxes, perhaps using them as blocks, and later decorate them with the tape. Nevertheless, the children focused more on the tape than on the actual boxes. Even though I had hoped to engage the children in a model-making experience, they showed me that their approaches to learning went elsewhere — in a perfectly valid direction. Veronica incorporated patterns, making long-short-long rows of tape. Kyra began writing on the boxes with a pencil she had found nearby in the art area. We were working in the block area, so we were able to spread out on the carpet. The pencil was not a backup or small-group material, and I thought it was neat that Kyra found it and thought to use it anyway. She already knew words like *mom* and

Children enjoy using this open-ended material with me outdoors.

dad, so it is possible she was labeling the boxes for people. Clyde worked on problem solving with the materials — he was trying to balance some boxes in position long enough so he could tape them together. He needed both hands to do this, as well as balance and control. He steadied the boxes between his legs as he worked on taping them. In the end, he had to really consider the shapes, angles, and size of the boxes to manipulate them the way he needed. Children are full of delightful surprises!

In talking about materials, I have some extra thoughts about the wood-working area. I will admit it: although I am not a worry wart, and I am not closed-minded, I will say that elements of the woodworking area took me by surprise for a bit. I thought it was so great that there was an area devoted to this type of construction. Seeing things like real wood, tools, things to take apart, and materials like sandpaper and glue was pretty inspirational.

So it's not that I didn't appreciate the authenticity of using the tools that my dad builds with in the garage or that my brother uses on construction sites (how amazing is it that the children can use the same materials and experiment with building and construction?!). Yet, it was a new concept to me to have real hammers and sharp nails in an area of the classroom used during work time (a time when teachers are ever-present partners in play but can be called away at times to support children in problem solving, for example). I have learned to stop asking myself "Why?" and begin asking "Why not?" instead. Hammers can be dangerous — but so can scissors, heavy wooden blocks, germs from the guinea pig, and bikes. Our classroom experiences are based on *active* learning. Why shouldn't the children be exposed to as many tools and materials as possible that they can manipulate in a safe and nurturing classroom environment?

Shannon acknowledges and supports children's choices in the woodworking area as these boys try out different ways to take things apart.

Philosophy

The HighScope philosophy, which is deeply rooted in active learning, adult-child interactions, and the consistency of the daily routine, are central to what I value most about early childhood education.

A number of people have approached me since I began this job just before HighScope's annual international conference in May. They have shared some thoughtful comments with me — those of encouragement and support. Teachers in the field wonder how I've handled the stress of jumping into a demonstration teaching position with sometimes more than 60 visitors per day (during conference week) after very little formal HighScope training. However, I don't think of it that way. Sure, it's been a new experience, and it was a bit nerve-wracking at first, but for me, the burden has been lifted. Throughout my teaching experiences, I have struggled with a grave disconnect between my personal philosophies on teaching and learning and those of most of the administrations with which I have worked. Certainly, at a few different schools, I had been teaching in a world where active learning is not valued. In fact, many of these experiences were with educators who were not aware of some of the most important issues in early childhood education. In some districts and programs, test scores are one of the main influences on teaching practice. Curriculum is decided upon haphazardly or in a purely teacher-directed fashion. Change is either restricted or else occurs repeatedly, restricting professional, student, and community growth.

Now I work in an atmosphere that expressly values research and lifelong learning and also facilitates supportive relationships among children and between children and adults while fostering exploration and curiosity through active learning. I know that a number of teachers still have to balance what they

The Five Ingredients of Active Learning

- Materials
- Manipulation
- Choice
- Child language, communication, and thought
- Adult scaffolding

know is in the best interests of children with decisions made by program, district, or state policymakers. But I know I'll always feel extremely blessed to have been a part of the HighScope team, and I extend encouragement, support, and pride to my colleagues in the field who continue to support early childhood education even when it seems as though their voices are not being heard. Such perseverance does not go unnoticed. These voices matter, especially to children.

Looking Ahead, Looking Back

What follows in the rest of this book are journal entries from my first full year of teaching at the Demonstration Preschool. Reflecting on my experiences and putting my thoughts down in writing helped me learn and grow, and I hope it helps you, too!

Positive adult-child interactions foster a joy for teaching and learning.

Chapter 2

Before School Starts

August

30

Tuesday

Home Visits

I'm getting back to my journal here just before the school year is about to begin again for the fall. Before school starts, we do home visits. This is a time when the Demonstration Preschool teachers go to children's homes so they can see children and parents interacting in their home environment. This helps us get to know the children and their families a little better, and they get to know us a little bit too! We can also give parents some tips for encouraging active learning at home when we interact with them during home visits.

Ideas and insights

Although this was not my first experience with home visits, it was my first experience with HighScope home visits. When I last taught preschool, at another center, home visits were mainly seen as an opportunity for children and teachers to play together and get to know one another. The parents were greeted and were present, of course, but they did not play an active role in the visit. However, during our HighScope home visits, I knew that it was important to share information with both the child and his or her parents. I really loved being able to share time with the parents and the children, including siblings, and thanks to my whirlwind introduction to the Demonstration Preschool last spring, I feel comfortable sharing information about the program with parents. Further, after each home visit, I found that picturing the visit in my mind helped me to remember the names of everyone in the family.

For the first time, I really understood the importance of every aspect of home visits. Spending this time outside of school with the children and their families is absolutely invaluable. Going to school, especially for the first time, can be a very intimidating experience for some children. It can also cause anxiety for parents. Providing the family with an opportunity to welcome the teachers into their home so parents and teachers get to know one another a bit, learn what to expect in the classroom daily routine, and share some things about themselves and/or their family life that they are proud of models shared control among children, parents, and teachers.

What did I observe about the children?

Some of the children were returning students and some were new to Shannon and me. Most of the children were thrilled to have us visit. Some of the children, especially new students, appeared shy and withdrawn at first, but it didn't take long for them to show us their home, bedroom, and toys. It was nice to see the children's backgrounds and interests reflected in what they talked about, their toys, and the and overall home atmosphere. Based on this, we were able to note certain interests that could help us make decisions about which materials to make available for children at the start of the year. For example, we noted that a few of the children enjoyed trains, so we selected the train set as one of the starting materials for the block area.

This mother and her children enjoy getting acquainted with the Demonstration Preschool teachers at their home.

26
Friday

Setting Up the Learning Environment

Ideas and Insights

When I came to HighScope in March, I was entering someone else's class-room. Even though I really enjoyed working with the children in that arrange-ment, and wouldn't have had enough understanding of HighScope's approach to setting up the learning environment to set up the classroom myself, I didn't quite feel like the classroom was *mine* or *ours*. So here in August, having the opportunity to set up the classroom with Shannon for the coming school year gave me a chance to practice what I had learned and to be intentional in my approach to teaching.

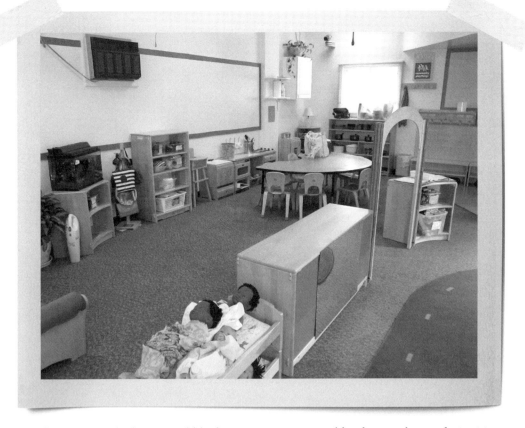

The furniture in the house and block areas are connected by the wooden arch, inviting children to move from one area to another.

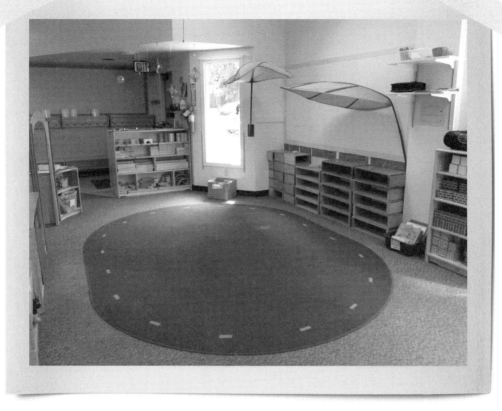

The block area houses various blocks and other building materials, trains, vehicles, and instruments that we rotate throughout the year. This space also serves as our greeting time and large-group time area.

What went well?

I'm a pretty visual person. I like to design spaces that are creative and aesthetically pleasing, as well as efficient and functional. Having the opportunity to start out with a clean slate was very motivating and exciting. I had some ideas about how to approach the setup of the classroom — from my own experiences and from the PCC training, which included watching the HighScope DVD *The Indoor and Outdoor Learning Environment.* Shannon, my teaching partner, was very thoughtful and supportive in helping me form ideas about how to create an inviting classroom.

Planning the block and house areas. We began with the house area and moved out from there. Shannon felt that keeping the block area and house area near one another was not enough — she wanted the play to be fluid between these two areas, and I agreed. In order to allow for the children to naturally move from the house area to the block area, we arranged the furniture to create spaces between these areas. In this way, we could encourage

This shelf in the toy area houses puzzles, people figures, and other items.

play that would develop and continue, especially within these two important areas. Later, we brought up the arch shown in the photograph on page 30. It fit perfectly in this space!

The toy area. We developed the toy area next to the block area, and these areas flow nicely together, from the large building materials in the block area to the smaller items like Duplos, animals, puzzles, and shells in the neighboring space.

The art area. We kept the art area in the tiled space near the sink. We moved some of the shelves as well as the sand and water table to make room for the easels, which we brought up from storage in the basement (we don't always have easels set up in the classroom, but we always have paint and paper available to children).

When we moved the sand and water table and the plastic floor cover beneath it, this allowed for the easels to share the floor covering. This change also gave a feeling of expanding the art area.

Children make drawings in the art area.

The book area. My main area of focus was the book area. I really wanted to create an almost *irresistible* space. To me, the book area is one of those
spaces in the classroom that can be nurtured and well-loved or ignored and
left to gather dust. Last year the children played in the book area, but I really
wanted to heighten the possibilities for experiences in this space. We brought
our couch, pillows, and bookshelf over to a corner to create the book area.
Using the stairs as an accent to this area really brought the concept together. A
rocking chair and some more throw pillows added to the cozy feeling of the
space, as did the lamp that was already secured to the wall.

On the other side of the book area (opposite the couch) the children
have ample writing space. So the book area has both a cozy feeling and plenty
of room for reading and continued play. Our plan is to add dimension and
texture with long, flowing, draped fabrics. And I would like the children to
have more spaces to crawl inside and underneath. I have fond memories of
climbing up and into spaces to read, rest, or just *be*. I remember feeling safe
when enclosed within magical "forts," dwellings, or other hiding spaces. (Of

The sand and water table rests between the toy and art areas. Plastic office-space floor mats are used to protect the carpet.

course, we want to make sure that we are able to see the children and that the space is safe).

More decorating and arranging. Some similar little touches really warmed the house area as well — a plant draping down from a high shelf, a framed photograph, a floor plant, and an armchair near the baby cradle. I also like having the fish tank in this space. We changed the curtains in the

This corner of the book area creates a cozy, inviting place for the children.

classroom to a bright yellow, and saved money by making our own (thanks, Mom!). The block area really brightened up with the large, nylon leaves arching over the carpet space (you can see them in the photo on p. 31). Perhaps these will encourage some forest play!

I'm a bit worried about the time (partway into the program year) when we will add computers to the book area and add the entire woodworking area to another part of our classroom space. Will I still feel as positive about our classroom setup, or will I think it feels squished? It's like anything else — as time progresses, it can become more and more difficult to keep it simple. I'll have to keep my focus in mind and come back to some of our original ideas in order to make sure that we are staying true to our plan for the space.

What didn't go as I had planned?

Our outside space is still something that we are working on. This is an ongoing process that is of interest to quite a few members in the HighScope Early

Another side of the book area allows for some big books, pillows, and a table of writing materials.

Childhood Department. Currently, our playground is a simple space with grassy, stone, and paved areas. We have a climber, a sandbox, a swing set, tree stumps, tree-ring pathways, a "crow's nest" (an elevated, wood platform built around a large tree) and a paved, subtle incline that the children run or ride bikes down. We also have many materials in our shed — some of which we may use in the classroom at other times. I would like to see the redesign of this space become our next project. We have been reading, perusing blogs, and just putting our heads together to come up with ways to make this space just as imaginative, inviting, and purposeful as our classroom.

What I Learned This Month

Here are some conclusions I've drawn from my own active learning experiences this month:

- Home visits can be a great opportunity to become acquainted with children and families. These simple visits can help children grow more comfortable with teachers and help the children know what to expect as school begins. Just as we support children through the transitions of the day, we can also help children to generally know what to expect when they cross the bridge from home to school.

- Setting up the classroom is a very personal, yet child-centered project. As teachers, it is one of our first opportunities to be mindful of our students and their needs and interests as we create spaces in which the children will work, interact, and play.

A view of the Demonstration Preschool classroom from near its entrance.

Chapter 3

Getting the Nuts and Bolts

Work in Progress

What Did I observe about the children?

I am beginning to see the newer children as expert *observers* in the classroom. Although they are new to the preschool and are still learning how the day works, these children take in their surroundings very carefully. There are so many elements of preschool life that are new for the children, and there are so many things for them to learn about. And yet, while we do try to prepare them for what will happen, we don't go over each little aspect of the day.

When the children began yesterday (after having been introduced to the teachers through home visits), we started as usual with a message board greeting. This introduced them to the events in the routine as well as to the other members of their groups, so they would know who would be joining them at their table. We will continue to go over the daily routine with the children at message board time at the beginning of each day. However, much of the rest of the day is left for pure *discovery*. It is fascinating to watch the children observe and explore their new surroundings. They begin to learn where they can find materials, how they can use the materials throughout various areas, and how to express some choices. These behaviors and activities reflect the children's engagement with the curriculum content category Approaches to Learning, and the following key developmental indicators (KDIs) in particular: KDI 1. Initiative, KDI 3. Engagement, and KDI 5. Use of resources.

Nikki is a child who is new this year, but she has comfortably adapted to our day (probably due in part to the fact that her sister had been here the past two years). Still, Nikki is learning how to make preschool a world of her own. She has discovered that using "work-in-progress" signs can extend a plan over a period of time.

Nikki has learned, by watching her peers, that if she uses one of these signs she can save her work and come back to it later. It was great to see this example of a child's engagement with KDI 45. Observing, from the Science and Technology curriculum content area.

Children use a work-in-progress sign to let others know they intend to return to working on their project another day.

What went well?

I approached Nikki in the toy area, where she had been building magnetic tile structures. She had two different constructions, and she was trying again and again to balance one "work-in-progress" sign across the tops of both constructions. After watching her struggle for a while, I went over to her and said, "It looks like you want to save two structures." She replied, "Yeah — I need another one [sign]." We both looked in the "work in progress" sign box together and saw that all of the signs were gone. "I wonder where we could get another one…" I began. Nikki wasn't sure. "Do you want to hear my idea?" I asked. "I wonder if we could make one," I continued. "Paper!" Nikki said, already thinking about what she could use. We talked about the color of paper she would use and what else she would need. She decided on yellow paper (to match the signs), and then she set off to get a pencil. She started by copying one of the existing work-in-progress signs. She was able to write the *o* in *work*, and then she asked me for

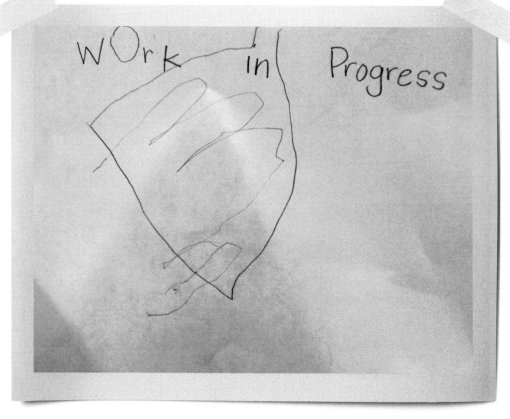

Nikki's completed work-in-progress sign.

help with the other letters. After helping Nikki with the words, I asked what else we could add. "I need a hand," she said. Nikki began tracing her own hand almost immediately. Then she encircled it to complete the "do not touch" message. She placed it on top of her structure and moved on to her next plan.

Ideas and insights

Since I began my teaching career, one of my main focuses has been to support my students in becoming independent. In the past, however, I may not have viewed the incident with Nikki as an opportunity for problem solving and writing but as an interruption to the child's play. However, after working with the children since March, I have come to appreciate their willingness to stick with a problem until it is either resolved or simply no longer a problem. What's more, I was pleasantly surprised with Nikki's determination to create an understandable work-in-progress sign on her own. After taking the time to problem-solve with the sole original sign, talk it through, make a decision, collect materials, and begin writing, Nikki had committed to this endeavor for about five minutes. When she finished, I could see the sense of satisfaction on her face. She moved to her next plan with that much more self-confidence.

September

15

Thursday

Recall Time

What went well?

Today was one of those days where I felt a bit frustrated with how some things went. But work time seemed to go okay, and by the time we got out-side, I really felt like things were back on track. The children were very en-gaged in their outdoor play, including everything from making potions in the sandbox, to chasing the evil witch, to swinging and biking.

What didn't go as I had planned?

Recall did not go well today. The overall engagement of children in the recall process fell short, even though I used a concrete strategy that is usually suc-cessful and I have been expecting only simple recalls from the children thus far in the school year. I know that it is the beginning of the year, but most of my children are returning preschoolers and should be capable of more. Today, I used one of the "go-to" recall strategies that I use when I'm having difficulty getting the kids into the swing of what we're doing: I asked the children to put a material that they used in a scarf and bring it back to the table. Nevertheless, today, children brought back their objects and played with them, in and out of their seats, noisily engaging in what seemed like almost a second work time. The problem was not that the children weren't "sitting still" or were holding on to their objects — I *like* to have the children hold something in their hands because it often helps them focus on what they are saying — but this time the material seemed to be a distraction. Also, I generally like the children to work together during recall time, but today they seemed almost oblivious of one another as they individually talked about what they did. When the children are truly engaged, they are often able to carry over their own experiences into the recall discussion of someone else's activities. When another child is recalling, they also often tune in and may share their own recollections of what that child did, whether or not they played together. In this way, the experience is shared, cooperative, and supportive.

Ideas and insights

While I do know that concrete recall strategies can be especially helpful for children who are still trying to develop the skills with which to review their work time, I wonder if the children would do better with something a bit more abstract. I would like to use a strategy that keeps the children actively engaged, yet allows for a connection to this part of the routine without the distraction. I am going to try giving the children a sheet of paper so they can draw what they did during work time. This way, the children will be able to

A child tells the group about the materials and other children with whom she played during work time. When using this turn-taking strategy, I give the children a baby animal to hold, and when I hold up the matching adult animal, that child knows it's his or her turn to recall.

actively participate (without waiting) as they reflect on their play. I know that this is a strategy that has children working independently; but I also know that, sometimes just after children have had a chance to express their own ideas, they will observe and comment on the others' ideas. Hopefully they will do this after working on their recall drawings. This could change again and again throughout the year, and that's okay. We are constantly adjusting and readjusting in the classroom — trying to keep to a routine, but manipulating certain elements so they fit the needs of the children.

September

21
Wednesday

What Are Pulleys?

What did I observe about the children?

Mason really got into the sand and water table today. While Miriam and Avery used the space for pretending with people figures, boats, and windmills, Mason was more interested in the movements of the water. He talked about what was happening to the water as it moved — how and where it fell, what happened when the colors mixed, etc. Looking up, Mason noticed for the first time the silver pieces attached to the top of our water table frame. "What are those?" he asked. "Those are for pulleys," I said. "What's a pulley?" Mason wanted to know. After I explained and vaguely illustrated how the pulleys would work, Mason was clearly fascinated. Although the pulley hardware was there, the pulleys were not yet set up for use — the ropes were still in storage. But Mason wanted to use them right then and there during work time. I admired this idea and tried to think of a way to incorporate the pulleys into his play while still maintaining a simple sand and water table for the beginning of the year.

The rope for the pulleys was downstairs. I started to tell Mason that we could use the pulleys tomorrow, but then I thought to turn the problem back to him. I asked Mason how we could use the pulleys if the rest of the materials were in storage for the day. What else could we use instead of the rope? This gave Mason the opportunity to make decisions about how this was going to work. Almost immediately, Mason blurted out: "String!" Although we didn't

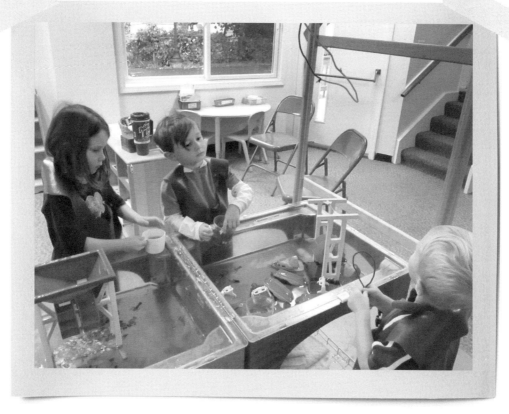

Children look on as Mason begins to construct a makeshift pulley.

have any string in the classroom, Mason marched right over to the art area and came back with some pipe cleaners in hand. My decision to allow Mason to take the lead led to further problem-solving.

What went well?

Once Mason retrieved the pipe cleaners, I reached up to help him attach one to the metal pulley, which was hanging from the frame of the water table. I asked him how he would like me to do this since he couldn't reach that high. We brainstormed what to add to this contraption: how would the water get down from up there? Mason thought, reached over, and turned back with a two-cup-size measuring cup in his hands. The handle was something that could hang over the pipe cleaner loop. After it was attached, we predicted what would happen with the water. When I got the cup up there I said, "I'm worried that this is still too high. The water might not fall into the table and you won't be able to reach it." We pondered how to allow the cup to be

Mason lifts the cup, which is full of water, using one hand to steady the cup and one hand to pull down the pipe cleaner part of the pulley.

moved down closer to the table. "More string!" said Mason. This pattern of collaboration continued as I helped by adding quite a few pieces of pipe cleaner until Mason could reach to help attach the last piece. Then he attached the cup to the lowest loop. His face lit up as he made the water fall from the measuring cup again and again.

Ideas and insights

Okay, I'll admit it. Although I would have probably seen this as an authentic learning opportunity in the past, I may have tried to control the situation a bit more. As I have mentioned, I've grown in my understanding of what it means to have *shared control* — but this is something I've had to work on to understand. What might I have done in the past? I could see myself dwelling on the fact that we'd kept the first weeks' sand and water table materials simple. But we did so for a reason — not to overwhelm children who didn't have much prior experience with the sand and water table.

Mason's idea inspired more exploration with pulleys the following day.

I could also see myself worried about a potential spill all over the floor (two cups worth, plus two cups worth, and then some). But I went over these things that may have bothered me in the past and brushed them aside. I asked myself, "What would happen if water spilled all over the floor?" And this answer came to me: Mason would problem-solve. He'd learn where the towels were. Maybe he'd feel supported as he collaborated with others to take care of it, or maybe he would independently take care of the problem and feel satisfied with his accomplishment. And, I wondered, why is it important for us to keep the water table simple if one of the children is already interested in something more complex? The moment Mason expressed an interest, I was hooked on his idea. I realized that the benefits of supporting his interest far outweighed any simple mishaps that may have come along.

The following day, we put rope on the message board to indicate that the pulleys were ready for use in the sand and water table. More of the children became interested in this aspect of water play. The conversations, queries, and delight continued as the children experienced a new facet of an enriched sensory experience.

September 26 Monday

Superhero Soup

What did I observe about the children?

We recently had Clyde and Declan (who were in two different groups) switch groups, with the hope that this would encourage the two boys to expand their plans and elaborate on their play. Both boys had been distracted by other children in their groups while making and beginning their plans. We wanted to give them an opportunity to start with some different children and see if new play partnerships would arise.

Even before this change, I had been working on my relationship with Declan. It has been difficult for me to engage in his play because he is very interested in superheroes and sometimes little else. It can be a struggle for both Shannon and me to step into his play because it often includes violent actions — for example, pretending to use weapons, pretending to die, and punch-

Important Notes

HighScope Groups

The HighScope Demonstration Preschool Classroom typically has 16 children and two head teachers. The children experience each part of the daily routine together, but some parts of the day (planning, recall, snack, and small-group time) are carried out in smaller groups, often at two tables in the classroom. That means each teacher is the *primary caregiver* of a group of about eight children, but he or she is also a whole-classroom teacher as well. The teachers share the responsibility of supporting all of the children throughout the day; but it's also important that the makeup of each group be carefully considered.

HighScope teachers consider the following when creating groups:

- The developmental levels of each child (some children are at earlier, middle, or later stages of development on a wide array of developmental characteristics, e.g., social-emotional, language, and mathematics development). We try to have a mixture of levels in each group.

- The ages of children and the amount of time children have already spent in the preschool classroom (our classroom has children aged three to five, some of whom are in their first year and some of whom are in their second year. Once in awhile, we have a child who is in his or her third year).

- The needs and interests of each child (including what teachers learn through home visits and other communications with families of children who are new to the program).

- Children's attachment to a teacher/caregiver (some children are naturally more drawn to a particular teacher, and teachers respect that when planning groups).

- How certain children work with one another. For example, children who often play together are sometimes put in the same group. Conversely, if there are children who often struggle or argue when together, the teachers may choose to separate them.

Every effort is made to keep groups consistent for at least three months; but sometimes children and teachers need a change, depending on how the considerations listed above play out.

ing or kicking into the air. Of course, I want to validate Declan's play choices. Also, pretending is an integral aspect of the curriculum — it is developmentally appropriate. But we've had difficulty supporting his plans and participating in his realm of the fantastic.

I desperately want to take on a role in Declan's play, but I also want him to be both safe and thoroughly engaged. His play often includes intense body movements such as kicking and running, but there really isn't ample space in the classroom for him to carry out these movements, even though this is something that his body needs. Moreover, this superhero play is sometimes limited by what the children know about superheroes from television. We've also been working on supporting the children in creatively adding new details to their plans. At this age, some of the children have seen superhero cartoons, but most of the children have a hard time imagining what superheroes actually *do*. So what happens in the classroom is that one child will begin superhero play, perhaps even assigning roles to others, but the children don't know how to develop their play. Declan's case is different, because he has spoken about watching plenty of shows that include superheroes; he knows who the superheroes are and how they move. Yet, he still doesn't quite know how to create a superhero scenario. It can be difficult for him to adapt his play, which would entail thinking about who needs help, and why, and what kinds of collaboration, tools, or props it might require.

During planning time, Shannon and I usually take the opportunity to encourage the children to elaborate on their plans. In this particular case (since Declan has experience with planning), we have decided that, if Declan plans to be a superhero, we will try to get him to extend the original plan by posing one or two leading questions or comments, such as "What does that look like?"; "What does a superhero do?"; "I wonder what kind of materials you'll use"; or "I wonder who you'll work with." This strategy hasn't always worked, but we see it as a starting point. Even so, we've found that the play can still "get stuck" because Declan has difficulty coming up with ideas other than just running back and forth across the classroom and punching a fist into the air. Of course, he is doing more than that, but again, extending this play to include more children and more active learning experiences is what we are hoping for.

What went well?

The start of today's work time led me to the book area, where Mina and Veronica were using the black race track, building it off of the stairs and adding ramps. Mason was looking for some race tracks to use, but half of them were already connected in the block area, and the girls had just gotten started using them in the book area. Mason came to me needing help with problem solving — he wanted to use the tracks, but they were all "used up." By the time we reached the girls, they were ready and willing to include Mason in their play.

That's when Declan stepped in to ask me for some help with his superhero cape. He wanted to tape a large piece of construction paper to his back, and he needed help with the tape. But before we cut the tape, I asked him if he wanted to write anything on his cape. Declan was wearing a Superman tee shirt, so, making a reference to a letter link, I said something like, "It looks like some superheroes have a symbol, just like we do," showing him the *S* on his shirt. "Yeah!" he said. What followed were some pretty exciting "learning moments" that included the following:

- ***Writing and dressing up:*** We worked on Declan's cape. He was so thrilled after successfully copying the letter *S* for *Superman*. "I did my *S* for my name!" he said. (He often struggles with those tricky curves.) Declan also made some pictures and letterlike forms, and handed them to me. "This is from the witch," he said. And he elaborated on how Superman would save people from the witch (Language, Literacy and Communication, KDIs 22. Speaking, 25. Alphabetic knowledge, and 29. Writing; Creative Arts, KDI 43. Pretend play).

- ***Engaging with others:*** "You're my kid," Declan said to me. "You are Supergirl and now I'm Fireman." At that moment, Kyra came over. "…And I'm your mom," Kyra said to me. "I'm gonna be Supermom, Supergirl!" continued Kyra. Declan agreed. Then Veronica and Mina approached: "Can we play?" Mina asked. "Yeah!" Declan said (Social and Emotional Development, KDIs 12. Building relationships, and 13. Cooperative play).

- ***Multiple areas:*** At this point, we had migrated from the book area over to the house area, with a stop in the block area to talk about some materials. Then Declan decided he needed to make some soup — Superhero soup (Approaches to Learning, KDIs 1. Initiative, and 3. Engagement; Mathematics, KDI 35. Spatial awareness)!

- ***Cooking:*** In the house area, Declan started mixing corks, poker chips, and rocks, telling me that these were soup ingredients; he added in some invisible ingredients as well. "Bubblegum, oil, and powder. You can add too much," he said. Declan stirred and stirred the soup. He talked about

Important Notes

Letter Links

Letter links is a name-learning system that pairs a child's printed name with a letter-linked picture of an object that starts with the same letter and sound: *F*lora and ❀, *S*am and ✄, *A*aron and ✈.

To be honest, when I first learned about letter links, I thought they were a bit silly. As an elementary and preschool teacher, I have seen the benefits of matching visual symbols to letters or words: children can make connections and understand more about the meaning behind the symbols in our alphabet and what they represent. But I wonder if they always make the connection. For example, how helpful it is to put a picture of a bird next to the letter Q? As adults, we can guess that it's a quail, but is it as helpful to children as we would like to think? I have worked with children who say "Q /qu/ — bird." But if handled appropriately, such examples can *help* children learn new vocabulary. For instance, my letter link, *Becky — banjo*, was an interesting one, because at first

the children thought the banjo was a guitar. Later, we observed how their understanding and vocabulary developed when it came up later in discussions about music, where I noticed they identified the instruments, and used the terms, correctly.

Fatima

Moreover, using letter links with the children in the High-Scope Demonstration Pre-school classroom has shown me how much they can add to the children's understanding of letter recognition, letter sounds, and the connections between these letters and the letters in children's (and adults') names. The symbols used (which are chosen by the children from a few given options) are very carefully matched to each name and its beginning sound or blend (a child named *Bree* would not have a butterfly letter link or a ball, but perhaps a bridge or bread). As the year progresses, the children begin to understand that certain pictures or symbols are connected to names.

Letter links are an effective teaching strategy because the pictures are more recognizable to young children than are letters. That is, it is more developmentally appropriate to use a symbol or picture than just a letter because letters are more difficult for preschoolers to recognize. Letters seem a bit arbitrary to young children (much as Chinese characters do to me). But once those characters or letters are connected to a picture, and even a name or person, children start to synthesize this information as they make connections in their brains. Therefore, a picture might start out as "Fatima's feather," but eventually children start to remark on the letters in Fatima's name as well — "That's Fatima's *F*!" Then children also begin to form small word or vocabulary banks organized by letters and sounds. So, when a child later decides to make a grocery list during work time, trying to spell the word *food*, he or she can link the words *food*, *Fatima*, and *feather* because of their shared beginning sound. Later, this literacy foundation will become the springboard from which children begin to read and write more and more.

Using nametags and letter links as labels in a variety of ways throughout the classroom and having children write their names to "sign in" each day engages children in a meaningful way with both phonological awareness and the alphabetic principle.

Declan writes a note from the "witch," setting the stage so that he, as Superman, can later save everyone from the witch.

what else he was adding to the recipe. "Pancake stuff and then juice and then you get some more there and then you get some more peppers, chocolate, milk, and beans" (Creative Arts, KDI 43. Pretend play; Science and Technology, KDI 50. Community ideas).

- ***Cleaning up as we go:*** After working so diligently in the house area with Kyra and me, Declan informed us that the "Evil Kid" was on his way. He was coming for us, but Declan didn't want him to find us. Declan said that even if we hid, the Evil Kid would find us, so we would have to flee. But I said I thought we'd have to hide the evidence before we could leave! Declan agreed, and so did the girls. We all cleaned up the area and fled back to the book area (Social and Emotional Development, KDI 11. Community; Creative Arts, KDI 43. Pretend play; Social Studies, KDI 55. Decision making).

What support do I need?

Last week, we had the privilege of hosting one of our HighScope board members, Amy Goerl. Although Amy had come to observe our classroom for various other reasons, we were able to speak with her a bit about her ideas for integrating more sensory experiences into our classroom and supporting the individual needs of the children. Amy has a special education background and, after observing, she shared some insights about the children's learning needs. Coincidentally, Shannon had just attended a session on sensory experiences in the preschool classroom, so she was also thinking about this.

The three of us sat down together to discuss some strategies to use with all the children, and we also brainstormed ideas for helping Declan. We discussed Declan as a "seeker," that is, he seeks out active learning experiences where he can express himself physically. So, we brainstormed some strategies that might encourage Declan to positively explore gross-motor experiences in his play. We thought of ways to help him have more of these experiences throughout the day, including encouraging such simple actions as carrying a heavy box to the outdoor area or throwing a ball into an area at planning time to indicate where he would play.

What I Learned This Month

Here are some conclusions I've drawn from my own active learning experiences this month:

- Children learn through observation, and multiage classroom environments help younger, newer, and/or earlier developing children (like Nikki, for example) to observe their peers, to learn more about the classroom, and to have unlimited discoveries. These children are then empowered with the knowledge and confidence to test out new theories and take exciting risks.

- Recall time can be challenging, but considering the many types of strategies (concrete or abstract, using props, games, or area representations) — along with the interests and needs of the group — is key to finding successful strategies.

- Sometimes teachers' intention to keep things simple can be challenged by children who are interested in pursuing things further and investigating a bit more deeply, as with Mason and the pulleys. While it's important to make plans and teach intentionally, it's also necessary to retain some flexibility to meet the challenges of the moment. We need to be ready to scaffold learning, which sometimes means we have to modify a planned strategy in order to support children at *all* developmental levels.

- Supporting children in their specific interests can become a very involved process (as with Declan's superhero play). Seeking support from colleagues and consulting other resources can help teachers find ideas for acknowledging children's choices and appropriately developing children's interests through a variety of curriculum-rich experiences.

Chapter 4

Growing Pains

October

4

Tuesday

Superheroes and Sunflowers

What didn't go as I had planned?

Today was tough. Work time's almost "dead end" superhero play has us questioning what to do next to help children extend this play theme. And recall time for my group is still an issue. Although the children *are* recalling, I don't think they are getting as much out of it as they could. It stills feels chaotic to me. Snacktime also felt that way to me today. Although snacktime is a social experience, and the children have rich language experiences while they eat, today children's voices became really loud at our table, and the children seemed to be feeling quite silly. I was reading a story to our group, and a couple of the children got out of their seats; others followed suit and ended up going under the table. I was unable to finish the story, disappointing those children who were listening. I could feel my ends unraveling. And large-group time — although sandwiched between manageable activities — fell apart after we brought out the song book today. The children were not engaged in singing, nor were they interested in practicing steady beat today. Several children were distracted, and they were talking and giggling with one another.

What support do I need?

Sue substituted for Shannon in the classroom today. It's always a joy to work with Sue; however, the children seemed to feel the change with Shannon's being out — they seemed less focused. After preschool was over for the day, I sat down with Sue to get some ideas. Talking through some possible strategies to use made me feel hopeful about the days to come.

I have found that it can be particularly helpful to brainstorm with a colleague who is very familiar with the classroom but has been removed from it for a while. It has become clear to Shannon and me that we need to change something to make the day run more smoothly for the children and ourselves. Sue has been able to provide ideas that we may never have come up with independently because we are always so caught up in what is *not* working.

This child counts the seeds that she has picked from a sunflower.

Another child uses a magnifying glass to take a closer look at the dried sunflower.

Since getting Sue's input, we have decided to think more about the dynamics of the two groups of children, to put out more materials in the classroom (including gloves, flashlights, and binoculars, which might help children elaborate on their "superhero" ideas), and to take to a look at the choices in the song book. We have even considered possibly taking a break from using the song book at large-group time.

What went well?

Small-group time with dried sunflowers. One part of the day today that *did* go well was small-group time. The activity was one that I had planned — exploring dried sunflower heads outdoors. I think that going to the outdoor space helped the children better engage with the experience after a hectic day. I introduced the children to the activity by talking about how we might use the magnifying glasses to help us observe something very closely. Then I showed them the dried sunflower heads that I had brought in, which my grandparents had saved for us to use. I wondered aloud what the children might discover when they took a look at the sunflowers. Some of the children wanted to discuss where the plants came from and what would happen if we planted some of the seeds. Some children ripped open the dried sunflower heads and felt the sticky substance inside. Others picked at the seeds with tweezers and fingers, sometimes counting the seeds.

October

5

Wednesday

Follow-Up to Superheroes and Sunflowers

Work time

Some children resumed superhero play during work time, but Shannon and I were vigilant — we challenged the children who took on any superhero or princess roles to build on the experience in new ways. As a result, Avery began enacting his superhero scenario by saying that he needed a flashlight to discover something. Miriam was interested in the flashlights too (these were recently added to the house area), and I jumped at the opportunity to

This child pulls the sunflower head apart, discovering the sticky, white flesh inside.

help her focus her plan. (Miriam had said that she wanted to be a superhero in the book area but that she didn't need any materials and was just going to get started). When Avery mentioned the concept of discovering something, I prompted both children to think further by saying "I wonder how you're going to know where to look when you *discover.*" When they weren't quite sure, I added, "Sometimes people use maps. Hey! Miriam drew a map yesterday. Maybe she could help you, Avery." They looked at each other and chimed their responses: "Yeah!" said Miriam as Avery said, "Come on," and they headed off to the art area.

Recall

Recalling by drawing what happened during work time went rather well today, especially compared to recall time yesterday. The children were very engaged, and the experience supported language through conversation, drawing, reading, and writing. Declan, Kyra, and Mason really got into copying children's

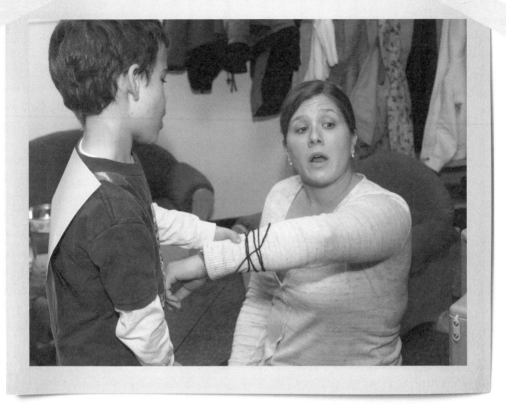

Rick the superhero pretends to untie me and save me from the evil witch.

names from name cards. Kyra had a list of three people with whom she had played, along with her picture. Then she began sounding out some of the letters she had copied! And Declan was so proud of himself after writing Veronica's name that he had to go right over to her table and show her! This was especially exciting because Declan sometimes shies away from writing opportunities, such as writing his name on the sign-up sheets, but I know he enjoys writing because he uses it to add to his play during work time (for example, by writing a note from "the bad guy"). I also used my strategy of asking them to bring back something they'd played with, and this time it really worked — I think it also helped children stay focused to have something in their hands. Looking back on my September 15 journal entry, "Recall Time," I realize that a strategy like this works better at some times than others — for a variety of reasons.

Large-group time

Large-group time both began and ended in a more focused way today. My group finished snack first, and I got right over to the carpet to begin an easy-to-join activity by singing "Aiken Drum," an 18th century Scottish nursery rhyme (see p. 64) that has been set to music by several artists. The children were able to take turns giving suggestions for lines and verses because we started with a smaller group — children trickled over from snacktime only one or two at a time today, which created a naturally fluid transition. I have found that when children have a smooth transition from snacktime to large-group time, they are more engaged during large-group time. Today we played "the freeze song," an activity in which each child starts and stops dancing on his or her own carpet square. When we were done, the children then unfroze one by one and put their carpet squares away to move to small-group time. We did not use the song book for this transition today, and I think this allowed us to keep the flow going at a point in the daily routine where things sometimes get scattered. Today things moved well.

This child elaborates on his superhero play as he uses props and attracts the attention of other children.

Important Notes*

Aiken Drum

There was a man lived in the moon,
Lived in the moon, lived in the moon.
There was a man lived in the moon,
And his name was Aiken Drum.

Chorus
And he played upon a ladle,
a ladle, a ladle.
And he played upon a ladle,
and his name was Aiken Drum.
And his hat was made of good cream cheese,
of good cream cheese, of good cream cheese.
And his hat was made of good cream cheese,
And his name was Aiken Drum.

Chorus
And his coat was made of good roast beef,
of good roast beef, of good roast beef.
And his coat was made of good roast beef,
And his name was Aiken Drum.

Chorus
And his buttons made of penny loaves,
of penny loaves, of penny loaves.
And his buttons made of penny loaves,
And his name was Aiken Drum.

Chorus
And his breeches made of haggis bags
of haggis bags, of haggis bags.
And his breeches made of haggis bags,
and his name was Aiken Drum.

*Children make choices of words to substitute in the different verses — for example,
"His eyes were made of blueberries" or "His nose was made of pancake."

October

12

Wednesday

"I'm Getting Used to You"

Ideas and insights

Today I spent some time reflecting on how things went yesterday — yesterday being probably the most challenging day so far this year for me. The children were especially rowdy, and the classroom dynamic just seemed off. Most of the children were interested in superhero play, but much of it didn't seem to develop. Problem-solving strategies seemed to fall just short of effective, and planning was again difficult to begin at my table.

Nevertheless, there are certain things we can do. Today Sue was substituting in the classroom for Shannon again, and we tried a few new strategies that seemed to go well. Here are some of the changes we tried today:

1. *We taped my letter-link symbol, the banjo (Becky — banjo), on the large chair in the cutout part our U-shaped table:* Children had been arguing over this seat anyway, and we thought that if I could perhaps sit more centrally in relation to all of the children (within arm's reach of each of them), that this would help with all of our group table times — planning, recall, snack, and small group.

2. *Carpet squares at large-group time:* We'd started using carpet squares earlier this week, and today we used the squares not only for the easy-to-join activity at the beginning of large-group time but also throughout the rest of large group. Having the children sit on their own carpet square enhanced their sense of personal space and body awareness.

3. *Recall time:* I wanted to give the children a new recall strategy that might also build on their interest in making and sharing multiple plans. At planning time a child usually makes one, two, or even three plans (for the different things he or she wants to do during work time, and classmates often join in with making and carrying out the first child's plans). Today at recall time, we used a recall wheel with the children's names on the various sections. We asked children to clip clothespins to the section(s) with the names of the children they played with.

What went well?

At this point in the school year, it feels very rewarding to begin seeing some of the children through a new lens. Last year I was with the children from the end of March until early June. In just over two months, I built relationships with all our students, of course, but I did not have the time to get to know the children in Shannon's group as well as the children in my group. Greater familiarity with three of the older children in particular — Declan, Miriam, and Avery — seemed to have eluded me last year. But now we are getting to know each other much better — and it's a wonderfully exciting process. Avery said to me today, "Becky, remember how I didn't talk to you a lot before? Now I do, 'cause I'm getting used to you." Growing with these children has helped me come to see their needs and interests more fully.

For example, I am learning that allowing Declan to move his body — (as long as he doesn't interrupt another's play) — is an important part of my interactions with him. Knowing that he approaches work time more physically than some other children do, we work on keeping him engaged and continuing meaningful connections and conversation. His work-time experiences also sometimes involve Miriam and Avery.

The scaffolding I do with Miriam at work time sometimes requires that I give her a gentle push to try some new materials. Today she said she wanted to be a mermaid in the book area, but that she didn't need any materials. I tried my usual next step — asking her what a mermaid does and trying to find out who else might be involved in her work-time plan. After talking about what a mermaid looks like (which involved Miriam moving back and forth, slithering on the floor), Mina became involved, and the girls made tails with paper, scissors, and tape. They cut paper pieces and wrapped them around each other's legs, then taped the pieces together. I still wonder why Miriam chose the book area — because it's a smaller area, the materials she needed were in the art area, and a lot of pretend play happens in the block and house areas. In our classroom, the book area is currently near the stairs (a small set of about four steps), which tend to attract the children. We also have a child-height, moveable archway, which often becomes the setting for acting out a fairy tale or two during work time. The next time Miriam chooses the book area for a pretend-play scenario, I'd like to muse out loud with her, "I wonder why you are choosing that area."

Miriam pretends to be a mermaid as she moves her "tail" back and forth.

19
Wednesday

A Maze for Valentine

Valentine, the class guinea pig, wrapped in his blanket.

What did I observe about the children?

Valentine is our class guinea pig. Sometimes the children make a work-time plan that involves Valentine. Such plans have included holding him, reading to him, or building him an enclosure in which to move about. I find it interesting that the children will sometimes gravitate toward this animal but at other times seem to completely forget that he is in the classroom — for days at a time! But I think this may not be unique to the guinea pig — it may be true for most of the classroom materials. The children do tend to forget what is available every day, perhaps especially at the beginning of the year. Even though we begin the year with fewer, simpler materials, there is still a great variety of materials available to the children. I think most often the children tend to make plans with their "tried and true" materials or areas, their favorite things, items that are most visible in the classroom, and/or the new materials that have just been presented on the message board.

What went well?

Today a number of the children made plans to build a maze for Valentine. It started with one child's having the idea and getting started, and it continued when a number of other children followed suit and subsequently spent the majority of work time in the block area working on this. Each child had different ideas for the maze. It began with Mason. He had a meticulous plan for how to begin building and what materials he would need in order to see his idea through to the finished product. Declan joined in, bringing additional big blocks over to the structure that Mason had begun. Mina began adding small blocks to decorate the outside of the maze, and Declan also got some newspaper to use as the floor of the maze.

Problem solving occurred as the children collaborated on the project, even though they had different ideas about the outcome. For example, Declan became frustrated when Mina put a large block on the inside of the maze because he couldn't lay down the newspaper "floor" with the block in the way. When I helped Declan and Mina practice the six steps to conflict resolution, step 4, restating the problem, proved particularly important to clearing up the misunderstanding. Meanwhile, Clyde joined in by adding more blocks, but Mason became upset because the blocks were "going the wrong way." Clyde, a more experienced problem solver, said, "I don't think he *knows* that I want to make it *turn*." When I restated that for Mason ("Clyde is saying that he wants the maze to turn toward a different direction here"), it made more sense to Mason. "Oh! Yeah!" he said. Thus, restating and clarifying the problem was important here, too.

As the maze grew, Declan continued to add newspaper for the floor as Liam, a younger child, watched. Miriam came over to see what was happening with the growing structure, and she added long, flowing pink fabric for decoration. Veronica touched it up with small "gems," or flat marbles, carefully placing them along the edges of the maze. When the children were finished with the main part of the maze, we brought Valentine out and placed him in the maze. Some of the children left the area — they had finished their plan —

The completed maze the children made for Valentine during work time.

while others joined with a new plan of petting and watching Valentine as he scurried about. Some children also added hollow blocks and made archways for the maze so Valentine had spaces to move through.

Building on what I already know

Last night we had a parent meeting, and our focus was active learning. This built on information we had given parents about key developmental indicators (KDIs) and other aspects of the HighScope Curriculum at the beginning of the year. Topics for parent meetings were chosen based on a survey given to parents on topics about which they might like to learn more. Last night Shannon and I discussed the five ingredients of active learning — materials; manipulation; choice; child language, communication, and thought; and adult scaffolding — elements that are a fundamental part of learning experiences in the HighScope Curriculum.

I reflected on the maze the children had built for Valentine in terms of the active learning opportunities the children had participated in. I concluded that the children were very engaged because they had a choice about which materials they would use and with whom they would work. They also had a wide variety of materials from which to choose, from all over the classroom, and they were able to manipulate these materials in the ways they saw fit. The children expressed their ideas through interactions with one another, as well as with the teachers. Children's conversation and language, like the construction of the physical maze they worked on, continued to build off of each active learning element they shared. Finally, as an adult involved in this scenario, I participated with the children in their play, having been invited to do so. Then, as a collaborator, I encouraged the children and used their ideas to scaffold their learning. I discussed with children what was happening as they thought of new ideas. I also imitated them — for example, adding big blocks when Declan added big blocks. I asked Clyde in which direction the next turn of the maze should go. I also encouraged the children to work together — for example, at one point I said, "I saw Veronica adding some of those gems too, Miriam. You could talk to her about how she did that."

Important Notes

Scaffolding Children's Learning

HighScope teachers strive to scaffold children's learning in their interactions with children, in conversations, and in small-group times so they can meet the needs of *all* learners in the classroom. That is, they support children at their current developmental level and offer gentle extensions to help children grow. They even add or change materials and the classroom setup to meet the needs of children, whether the children are at earlier, middle, or later stages of development in a particular area.

The HighScope Demonstration Preschool is a classroom for children aged three to five, but regardless of whether a setting teaches three-year-olds, four-year-olds, or various ages, children in any preschool have different needs, styles, backgrounds, and interests. This is why differentiating for each child is such a key aspect of scaffolding the children's learning. In some ongoing ways, HighScope teachers scaffold as they set up the classroom in

the following ways: planning for groups that include children of various developmental levels (e.g., mixing children who are new to the classroom with more experienced children so the less experienced children can learn from the more experienced ones), supplying materials that engage children of various levels (for example, both simpler and more complex puzzles), engaging the children's diverse interests (knowing that having a variety of interesting materials and interest areas can spark children's interests in multiple ways), and labeling the classroom (with pictures, words, or other representations) to help children find the things they are interested in.

Teachers also sit down together and plan for daily scaffolding opportunities, writing these ideas down so that they can be even more mindful of carrying out their plans. They plan large- and small-group times, and think about how the children might engage with materials and one another. They plan for transitions that will help all the children move smoothly from one part of their day to the next. They also plan for using materials that are open ended so children can choose how to manipulate them.

What is more subtle, but just as powerful, is the way that

HighScope teachers scaffold children's learning spontaneously as they interact with the children throughout the entire day. Scaffolding is about *planning activities* to reach all children — yes! — but it is also about strong and positive adult-child interaction strategies that extend language skills, acknowledge children's choices (for example, by imitating what the children are doing, when possible, and by challenging their thinking or extending it further). What this might look like during work time, for example, is that a teacher will join in a child's block-building play, acknowledging the child's choices of block size and his or her decisions about how to stack them (thereby beginning a conversation about the child's work), and finding ways to challenge and extend the child's thinking (perhaps referring the child to other materials or children who might inspire the child to develop his or her work further). The guinea pig maze is an example of how children can elaborate on their play in a collaborative way.

26
Wednesday

The Big Box

Ideas and insights

Recently one of our departments purchased a new copy machine. Exciting, right? But it was! It was as if the big box that the machine had come in had just been waiting for the children to discover it and figure out what to do with it! When we showed the children the box today, we didn't know what they would do with it, of course, but we had indicated on the message board that the box was in the classroom and figured we would just go from there. As I'm sure I've mentioned, one of the most valuable lessons I've learned from using the HighScope Curriculum is to put more control into the hands of the children when introducing a new material or activity. In this case, we considered the many creative-thinking and problem-solving opportunities the box might offer the children — that is, how they might work together to decide what it was, how they could make room for more kids to fit inside the box, and even how they might orient and manipulate the box (horizontally or vertically, flaps up or down, flaps secured with tape, etc.).

What did I observe about the children?

Many of the children were interested in the box, especially after we set it up three-dimensionally (we had flattened it out for storing), and kids began to think about what the box could be used for. During their first experience with the box, the children were excited about climbing in and out of it. The box was rather high, which made it impossible for the children to swing their legs over the side without assistance. Declan decided to stack a large block next to the box, but it was still a bit of a stretch to climb in. Mason grabbed another block and placed it on top of the one Declan had brought over. Now the step itself was becoming too high, so Clyde added a new step below the first one. Soon the children had a small staircase for climbing up into the box. Working alongside the children and acknowledging their choices, I encouraged the children to take the lead. When they had difficulty reaching their legs down into the box, I suggested another block on the inside. Then the pretend play began. Before we knew it a "tornado" was coming, and everyone in the block area had to climb into the box! Miriam covered us up with a sheer pink fabric because everyone knows you need a roof when a tornado is coming!

Mason uses the stairs that he and other children built to climb over and into the box.

More children attempt to climb into the box with me after Miriam has added a fabric "roof."

October

28

Friday

Reflections on "The Big Box"

What did I observe about the children?

As the days continued, we were able to create various experiences with the box throughout the daily routine, building on the children's interest in it. Shannon's group used the box for planning time, and my group used it for recall. We also used it as a boat for large-group time, and we sang a song as we "rowed."

The box continued to take on a number of roles during work time. Superheroes used it as their hideout, and families called it home. Clyde started

*This child rows the boat during large-group time as all the children recreate
a nursery rhyme.*

While the children are sitting in their "house," I read a story that Kyra has chosen.

dropping marbles through the slits in the cardboard on the sides of the box. Nikki watched and collected the marbles as she and other children explored their movements. Later, several of us climbed in and out of the box and laid down on blankets and pillows inside. With the box flipped on its side and some of the children sitting inside and others, outside, I read a book the children had brought to this "house." Later, Kyra went into the box as she pretended to feed her baby and put her to bed. Then she said it was time to watch television. When I asked her where the TV was, she said, "I'm the TV!" Then she deepened her voice and said, "Hello, today it's the weather, and it's sunny. Tomorrow it's going to be not sunny!"

Shannon brought in another box for the children to use at outside time. I watched Finn and Liam climb inside and beg to be covered up so that someone could open the box and find them. I saw other children climb in and out, then add wheels to it and pretend to drive off for an adventure!

What I Learned This Month

Here are some conclusions I've drawn from my own active learning experiences this month:

- Adding props and resources to the classroom that match children's specific interests can help the children extend their play, encourage them to collaborate with one another, and help them become more detailed in their plans and work.

- As the year progresses, the time that adults spend with children naturally adds more to the classroom experience. That is, children's growing comfort level in the classroom environment, and with adults and one another, fosters positive social and emotional development and growth in other curriculum content areas. I've observed that the children's play is enhanced as children become more comfortable sharing and expressing social, emotional, and language experiences.

- Pets in the classroom are for active learning too! Together, most of the children in the classroom had some role in collaboratively developing a space in which Valentine could move. Providing a space for the animal gave the children a collective goal, and they worked together as a community to create this.

- New, recycled, and unusual materials (such as the box) provide exciting and unique opportunities through which the children pursue their own interests and investigate different parts of their world.

The children experiment with the box outdoors: putting "loose parts" in and taking them out and then climbing over the log to get inside the box to hide.

Chapter 5

Hitting
My Stride

November

1

Tuesday

TAPE!

What went well?

Many of the children have become engrossed in activities involving ramps, tracks, inclines, cars, and other vehicles. Yesterday, Clyde and Mason spent most of work time driving cars down plastic race tracks that they had taped to the shelf. The children talked about the cars' speeds as well as the distances they traveled. I wanted to try a small-group activity based on this interest while encouraging the children to compare and measure.

The children were delighted to get their hands on the new rolls of colored masking tape we had in the classroom today. I introduced the material as something different they could use for making roads, and the toy cars were the backup material. (The backup material allows us to extend children's learning as needed. We want the children to have ample time with the initial materials before we bring out the backup material.) The complete small-group activity I designed is shown on pages 82–83.

Important Notes

Small-Group Activity: Tape on the Floor

In this small-group time, the children stick various lengths of colored masking tape on the floor to make roadways for small cars. (See photo on p. 84.)

Originating idea: At the HighScope Demonstration Preschool, groups of children have spent much of work time driving cars down tracks, comparing speeds of different cars, and using inclines to change their paths. Based on this interest, I chose this small-group activity to encourage children to use comparison words and measurement terms.

Materials:

Materials for each child and teacher:

- Roll of colored masking tape
- Scissors
- Basket to hold above materials

Shared materials:
- None

Backup materials:
- Small cars

Key developmental indicators (KDIs):

Mathematics — KDI 35. Spatial awareness: Children recognize spatial relationships among people and objects.

Mathematics — KDI 36. Measuring: Children measure to describe, compare, and order things.

Beginning (how you introduce the activity):

- Have the children join you in an open space on the floor in your classroom. (We used the carpeted block area, the same space we use for large-group time.)

- Begin by introducing the materials or describing what prompted this activity. I began with talking about what prompted this activity: *"Yesterday I saw Declan and Mason building long roads for their cars at work time. Today we have a new material that we could use to make long and short roads."*

- Give each child a basket with tape and scissors and say "I wonder what kinds of roads you will make."

Middle (how you support and extend each child's learning):

- Observe how the children are using the tape and scissors. Acknowledge their choices, and imitate their actions. *For example, in my group, Miriam used the red tape to make roads of various lengths. I commented, "Miriam is making some long roads and some short roads." She replied, "And some medium!" when she added a third piece.*

- If children choose to use the materials in other ways, support their ideas as well. *Veronica taped her basket and made a handle. I asked Veronica how she did that and then followed her steps to make the handle as she told me the sequence.*

- Introduce the cars once children have spent some time sticking tracks on the floor. Continue to talk descriptively about what children are doing. *For example, "Liam is adding tape to his long, blue road" or "Clyde is driving his car across the yellow road."*

End (how you end the activity and transition to the next part of the routine):

- Remind the children when they will have about three minutes left of small-group.

- As children finish, ask them to sort their materials — tape in one basket, scissors in another — as part of cleanup.

- Remind children that they can resume using the materials at work time and/or that the colored tape will be available for use in the classroom the next day. *I told the children in my class that the tape would stay on the carpet all week.*

- Ask each child to walk along a road on the floor as they transition to the next part of the daily routine.

Ideas for follow-up or related activities:

- Put a message on the message board reminding children that the tape will stay on the floor for the week so they can use it throughout the day. (*Note: We found the masking tape does not damage the carpet. The tape remained on the floor in our classroom for an entire week and did not affect the carpeting, even with daily vacuuming.*)

- For planning time, add classroom area signs to the various parts of the carpet "roadmap" (made from the masking tape). Ask each child to drive a car to the area in which he or she plans to work.

- If the children are still interested in the floor tape, use the materials in another small-group time. Have the children add to the lines or roads, and give each child a measuring tape to measure different lengths of masking tape on the floor.

What did I observe about the children?

As I've now come to expect, all of the children used their materials in slightly different ways, which is completely appropriate. Mason connected his tape to mine and shouted, "We're making roads!" Then, almost immediately, he incorporated my backup material: "Hey, let's get the cars!" he said. However, because I wanted children to have as much experience as possible with the new material first, I encouraged them to continue focusing on the tape before I got out the cars.

Veronica began by pulling off long strips of tape. She lined them up, one next to the other, saying "A medium one, a small one, and then a big one." Kyra made a basket handle with her materials, attaching the colored tape to the basket I'd used to hold individual sets of materials. Veronica tried the same. The girls were excited about their creations, and indeed, I had never thought that creating and building would come into this lesson. Problem solving with materials was another important part of the process. The children had

The children problem-solve while exploring measurement, lines, and shape during this small-group activity using colored masking tape.

already had some experiences with tape, but they were still finding it tricky to pull up the edge of the tape, and to hold and manipulate the scissors while also handling the tape. Veronica's tape twisted around itself, and she couldn't get it to unravel. "I messed it up," she said, trying to pull the tape back apart. Kyra put tape on a box that was lying on its side in the block area, but she couldn't hold both the tape and the scissors. She asked Veronica to help her cut the tape. Veronica joined in, exclaiming to Kyra, "I love the colored tape! Cover the [box's] letters!"

In the end, tape was going in different directions — overlapping, starting and stopping in many places across the rug — and most of the children had begun working together to add more tape to the box and to the floor. This became a rich opportunity for both language and social experiences. Mason started to notice the shapes of the tape lines, saying to me, "I knew you made a *K!*" Veronica found an *X* someone had made, and Kyra pointed out a *Y.* Clyde said his tape lines looked like a triangle, and Miriam described her lines as growing "longer." "We're taping everything in the block area!" Kyra said. And later she added, "I taped my own shirt! My mom might laugh!"

Building on what I already know

As I reflect on today's small-group time, I note how I observed the children, acknowledged their choices, and imitated their actions. For example, in my group, Veronica used the red tape to make roads of various lengths. I commented, "Veronica is making some long roads and some short roads." To this she replied, "And some medium!" while adding a third piece of tape. And when children chose to use the materials in other ways, I supported their ideas. For example, when Kyra attached tape to her basket to make a handle, I said, "Kyra is adding tape to her basket. How did you do that, Kyra?" Then I followed her steps in sequence, as she told me what she had done. Throughout small-group time, I continuously spoke in descriptive terms about what the children were doing, with comments such as the following (descriptive language in italic): "Clyde is *adding* tape to his *long, blue* road" and "Declan is *driving* his car *across* the *yellow* road." I didn't introduce the cars (my backup material) until near the end of this small-group time — and the activity was going so well that it would have been fine even if I hadn't brought the cars into it.

I think what made this small-group time so engaging was that the material was new and yet familiar — the children had used masking tape before, but not the colored tape we used today. The children were enthralled with the idea of using as much tape as they needed and taping it wherever and however they saw fit (though I did redirect some children who had started putting tape on blocks in the block area, as I was concerned the tape wouldn't come off the blocks very easily).

Follow-Up to "TAPE!"

Ideas and insights

Because the children were so excited about the masking tape activity yesterday, I adapted this idea for another small-group time and for planning time

Area sign designating the classroom book area.

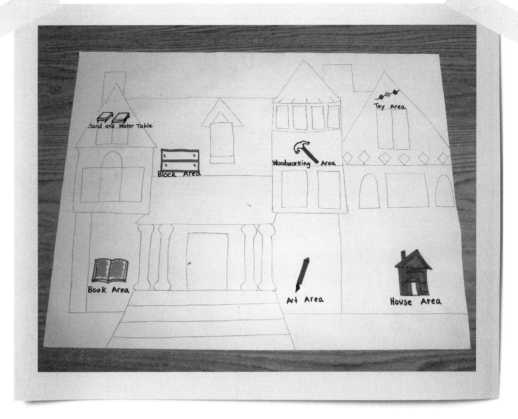

"Area signs" on this poster help children plan where they want to work.

today. For planning time, I added area signs (signs designating the different classroom learning areas) to various parts of the carpet "road map" that the children made with tape yesterday, and each child drove a car to the area in which he or she planned to work. Today's small-group time using the tape had a focus on measurement. In this activity, I scaffolded children's learning with measuring tapes as the children continued to add tape to the floor. The children had previously used measuring tapes in other small-group experiences, but this time we used flexible sewing tapes instead of retracting, metal measuring tapes. This was a new twist on a material that the children had already found interesting. In addition to measuring with the sewing measuring tape, some children compared the sewing tape to the masking tape on the floor.

More Follow-Up to "TAPE!"

What did I observe about the children?

Today Shannon's group tried the tape and measurement activity for small-group time in the far end of the classroom. They added position and direction words to their focus as they taped *up, down,* and *across* the stairs.

We have decided to keep the two groups' masking tape on the floor so the children can continue exploring with it during work time. We have put a message on the message board reminding children that the tape will stay on the floor for a week or so. [*Editor's Note:* By the end of the second week, the tape was removed from the carpet with no problems, even after daily vacuuming.] I feel excited that we have been able to further the enthusiasm that began with one small-group activity; it really has given the children a chance to fully explore the tape. I noted that the KDIs children engaged with on the second and third days were the same as they were in the first small-group activity with the tape; even though the children used measuring tools in the second activity, the previous day they had used measurement terms, so KDI 36. Measuring applied to both.

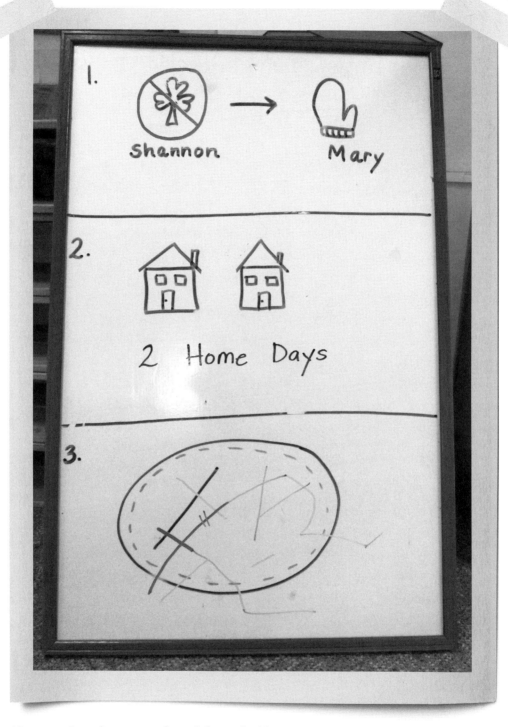

Message #3 on the message board shows the blue rug covered in colored masking tape. During greeting time, the children and adults talked about the tape on the floor, and the children understood that the tape could stay on the floor to be used during work time.

Throwing and Retrieving Balls

What did I observe about the children?

A number of the children were interested in using balls today. During work time, some of the children used balls in the block area. Declan, Clyde, and Miriam threw the crochet balls and watched them hit the wall and fall down into the hollow blocks. They threw them up over the large, nylon, decorative leaves we have up (see photo on p. 31), which serve as a canopy over a portion of the block area.

While doing this, Declan, Clyde, and Miriam were laughing together and trying to throw the balls higher and higher. They predicted where the balls would fall and counted how many balls they were throwing.

At outside time today, a few different children threw balls from the train climber. Liam had begun to show interest in the smaller, bouncier balls, and before we knew it, he had taken the whole tub of balls up on the climber. I commented on his actions. As we both began to throw balls from the train, I talked to him about watching out for other children so they wouldn't accidentally get hit with the balls. Soon Mason and Finn joined in. The boys talked about the balls (using words and phrases like *big, smaller, squishy, bouncy,* and *looks like a tomato*) as they meticulously chose each one and threw it, comparing the distances thrown. Liam, Mason, and Finn then took turns choosing and throwing a ball, watching it soar, laughing, retrieving the ball, and beginning again. Quickly, however, the speed at which they would acquire the ball and then set it free became a new component of the game — they would throw all of the balls out of the bucket as quickly as they could. Then Liam, Mason, and Finn would run down the steps of the climber and out to collect all of the balls, and this process would quickly begin all over again. I watched the three boys engage in this series of actions four or more times.

Building on what I already know

It was an interesting happenstance that two different groups of children chose to work with balls at two different points in the day. It's possible that the younger boys (Liam and his friends on the train climber during outside time) were inspired by the ball throwing that they had seen from their older peers during work time — or else they were simply interested in that material today. Regardless, *I* was interested in the parallels, and in the imitation and adaptation of experiences that were happening indoors and outdoors. Near the end of the morning, as the children threw the balls outdoors, watched the balls move across the playground, ran to get them, and returned to engage in this action again and again, I knew the children were doing more than just enjoying their outside time — they were also engaging in many layers of learning! As I looked at some of the anecdotes that I'd written down, I was able to record evidence of connections to some KDIs:

- *A. Approaches to Learning, 1. Initiative: Children demonstrate initiative as they explore their world.* Children engaged in play, materials, and play with one another.

- *B. Social and Emotional Development, 12. Building relationships: Children build relationships with other children and adults.* Children engaged in and sustained interactions with one another.

- *C. Physical Development and Health, 16. Gross-motor skills: Children demonstrate strength, flexibility, balance, and timing in using their large muscles.* The children threw the balls and moved up and down stairs and across the playground.

- *D. Language, literacy, and communication, 23. Vocabulary: Children understand and use a variety of words and phrases.* The children described the balls and talked about what was happening.

- *G. Science and technology, 45. Observing: Children observe the materials and processes in their environment. 46. Classifying: Children classify materials, actions, people, and events.* The children described and compared what the balls looked and felt like, as well as how far and where they traveled. They used position and direction words in their conversations.

These notes will prove useful when we do our Child Observation Record (COR) evaluations. (I have learned that it is also important to compare COR items to the relevant KDIs for an activity.)

All of these learning opportunities came from such a simple material (the balls), and they were all based on the children's *interest* — something they *chose* to engage with during work time and outside time.

Follow-up

I thought of other strategies I could use for working with the children's interest in balls: crochet balls are a good indoor movement choice for children who seek a more physical activity, as are beanbags and other soft balls. Also, we have used foam balls with buckets for large-group time and/or during an indoor "outside time" when we couldn't go outdoors because of the weather.

I plan to use the crochet balls in the classroom for recall time tomorrow. I will ask each child to throw a ball into the area where he or she played. For outside time, I'll make a point of taking balls of various sizes, shapes, and textures out of the storage shed for children to use.

A small-group-time lesson that I really enjoy, and may try later this week, is bowling with paper towel tubes and soft balls. I have adapted this particular small-group time from HighScope's Numbers Plus Curriculum — from Number Sense and Operation, activity 4: "Bowling and Beanbags." (I modified the activity by not using the number cards that this activity mentions). Here's how the activity goes: The children are each given about eight paper-towel tubes and a ball. The tubes are set up on their ends like bowling pins, and the children try to knock them down by rolling a ball into them. The focus of this activity is on counting. For example, I count and say, "I have eight tubes, and I'm going to see if I can knock some down." After some are knocked down, I count and say something like "I knocked down one…two. Let's see how many I have left…."

This is a great activity for incorporating counting, motor skills, overall body awareness, and other KDIs.

15

Tuesday

Crinkled Paper in the Art Area

What didn't go as I had planned?

Today we rotated into the art area a material that the children hadn't used yet this year — small strips of crinkled paper. Last year the children attending the Demonstration Preschool used this material in a variety of ways, including gluing the strips to paper and other art materials and stirring them into mixtures they "cooked." We introduced this new material on the message board by simply taping it to the board next to a drawing of the art area sign. We had wondered how the children could use it, and many of them said that they would use glue with it. What happened during work time was quite interesting. Shannon used the word *confetti* when introducing the material to the children, and it became apparent that this was a word they knew — for, once they heard her use that word, the children changed their idea of how to use the material entirely, as I describe below.

What did I observe about the children?

As often happens during work time, a number of the children were preparing for a "party" in the block area today. They began by using large, hollow blocks to build a house and table. Some of the children continued to stack blocks while others went to the house area to start "cooking" in the kitchen. Before we knew it, the block area housed a stage (made from more large blocks), a castle, and all the fixings for a party; soon, invitations and food items were strewn about. Mason walked over with a platter of play dough filled with Popsicle sticks — perhaps to represent candles. The children asked if we could put some music on so they could start dancing — and before we knew it, Kyra had retrieved the crinkled paper and started tossing it into the air while dancing around. A few more children joined in, and I started to see the action in the block area unfold before me as if in slow motion.

Building on what I already know

As the children started tossing the confetti in the air, the first thought that came to my mind was: "Oh my goodness, this is going to be a big mess!" I tried to think about how to minimize the mess without limiting children's exploration of the material. That is, I didn't want to be directive and take over the children's play. However, I also didn't want to let this become a *laissez faire* scenario. I thought about how, if some parents had walked through the door at that point in our work time, they may have seen only chaos! As I came to a decision about how to respond to the situation, I thought it probably *looked* somewhat careless; however, my response to the situation was driven by intentionality.

I acknowledged the children's actions and choices. For example, I said, "Wow, Kyra is using the confetti to celebrate at the party. You're excited about that!" However, I also made sure to express my concern, so the children would know how I was feeling: "You know what?" I started, getting down on the children's level and stopping their play for a moment, "I'm worried that if we continue to spread the crinkled paper all around the block area, it will take us a long time to clean it up." But clearly, the children didn't share my concern, or naturally, my foresight. In fact, Kyra was so caught up in the moment that she continued to spread more and more confetti, squealing in delight as she ran around the carpet sharing this joy with other children.

At this point I had already decided that we would all have to talk about this situation retroactively, and that the children would benefit from the learning that would stem from the natural consequences that would soon arise (i.e., that cleanup would take a long time and/or that outside time would be shortened). This was something that I was okay with, and I felt that the learning that might come from this would be more useful than stopping them at the height of their play, especially as so much of the "confetti" had already been spread on the floor. Thankfully, we were nearing cleanup time. The children had already received the five-minute reminder signaling that work time would soon end.

As cleanup began, we grabbed children's attention by dimming the lights and asking the children to reach up high and then down low. While we still had their attention, I said, "We have a lot of material to clean up today; we are going to need your help, especially in the block area. How will you clean up today?" As the children were sharing how they would move their bodies (for example, clean like a robot, carry things in their shirts, scoop up blocks like a

Important Notes

Intentional Teaching

I first began to really think about intentional teaching when I was studying early childhood education in graduate school. In a number of my courses, I can remember learning and talking about the importance and impact of intentionality. I had a good grip on the concept, but HighScope taught me both the bigger picture and the finer details.

All teachers plan ahead and have good intentions to implement their curriculum in various ways. But true intentionality — what I think of as *the art* of intentional teaching — runs much deeper. In HighScope classrooms, teachers plan how and when to scaffold children at their individual level. Teachers anticipate what the children might do and then describe what they think they may see or hear the children do. HighScope teachers also intentionally plan for specific environments, routines, areas, materials, group times, messages, and transitions that will support children, facilitate learning, and structure positive experiences in appropriate and meaningful ways. HighScope teachers also reflect on and discuss these intentions and assess what to add or modify.

crane, etc.), I pulled Kyra, Mina, and Veronica aside and said, "We have a lot of crinkled paper on the floor. I wonder what we can do about that." Before I knew it, the girls were using buckets, brooms, and whatever they could manage to pick up the pieces. Cleanup did take a long time, and the children even talked about that at recall time. At snacktime, the crinkled paper came up yet again; we had a long talk about how much time it took to clean it up, and I mentioned the natural consequence that would ensue — that outside time would be shorter than usual.

November 16 Wednesday

Follow-Up to "Crinkled Paper in the Art Area"

What did I observe about the children?

Today, Shannon and I took the opportunity to address yesterday's crinkled paper mess on the message board. We drew a picture of the blue carpet with squiggly colored lines all over it. A question mark was drawn beside it. As they read this symbolic message, the children were prompted to think about how they had used the crinkled paper the previous day. We talked about the problems we'd experienced and shared the feelings we'd had. Some of the children said they had felt frustrated that cleanup time had taken so long. Some children said they had felt sad that outside time had had to be shortened. We even talked about the extra paper that the teachers had had to pick up at the end of the day because pieces were still on the carpet. We also discussed solutions together and agreed that the crinkled paper was a material that the children could use in the art area. We asked the children, "How could we use the crinkled paper?" "We could glue it!" Clyde said. "Hey, I know! We can tie it to things!" said Miriam.

Ideas and insights

For me as a new HighScope teacher, the crinkled paper activity was a good experience from start to finish. Even though part of me had wanted to immediately stop the children from scattering the confetti, guiding children through the natural consequences (and recalling it together the next day) was far more valuable for all of us than it would have been if I'd tried to stop a storm of enthusiastic play that was already underway. The paper had been scattered immediately. The bottom line was that I had not wanted to limit children's use of a material. But stepping in to guide the children (including discussing appropriate choices for use of the material) really seemed to support our community of problem solvers.

What I Learned This Month

Here are some conclusions I've drawn from my own active learning experiences this month:

- Truly engaging experiences, such as the masking tape small-group time, can become a springboard for further activities that build on the children's initial excitement and understanding, to foster extended and more elaborate play.

- When children engage in seemingly simple play (throwing and retrieving balls, for example), a world of learning can actually be taking place — across all aspects of the curriculum.

- Allowing children to experience challenging feelings and natural consequences (for example, in the crinkled paper situation where cleanup time cut into outside time) can facilitate strong learning experiences for the children, if handled in mindful ways.

Important Notes

Keeping a Teaching Journal

Ever since my student teaching days, I have strived to maintain the practice of self-reflection. Teachers who reflect on their practices are better able to monitor their own professional development, celebrate successes, learn about challenges in order to seek support where needed, and assess the teaching and learning that is taking place in the classroom. Holding discussions with colleagues, mentors, and other professionals in the field is a great way to get started in the process of reflection. However, I have found that the additional step of writing really helps me to process my thoughts and keep feelings, reactions, and questions in the present.

Here are some tips to consider:

- **Take time to debrief:** Set aside time each day or once a week to write about things that really stand out in your teaching experience. I had originally planned to write journal entries from my daily notes twice a week, but I ended up changing my goal to once a week — it is more practical for me, and it makes my writing more meaningful. I write about things that really strike a chord with me, and I think that doing so has made my insights clearer (writing when inspired, rather than writing for writing's sake).

- **Talk to colleagues:** As mentioned above, working through ideas with others in the field is an important part of the reflection process. I have found that doing this can really foster support and collaboration. I have also realized that, no matter what the challenge in a school setting, I can usually find at least one or two teachers who are struggling with the same issues that I am. Talking through my experiences with coworkers has helped me feel understood and supported. Additionally, when working with partner teachers or classroom support staff, discussing classroom highlights and student development are integral to effective planning. When keeping a journal, you can add highlights from these conversations to your writing.

- **Read the ideas of others:** Use resources such as books, websites, DVDs, and trainings to find out what others are doing in the field of early childhood education. Be sure to check out blogs as well! Find a couple of educators to follow. They may spark your interest in blogging yourself. They also can serve as models for how to start or maintain a teaching journal.

- **Find a voice:** As keeping a teaching journal is a form of active learning, you have choices in how to reflect! Find a layout or style that works for you. Use a notebook or type your ideas. Take pictures, if your program allows for it. When I don't have time to fully develop a journal entry, I jot quick notes and use pictures to add to the documentation until I can add more to it later.

- **Read what you write:** After a while, go back through your ideas and skim for patterns. If there were things that you were struggling with before, have you implemented new ideas? Have you improved?

Chances are that you have improved, and you have different challenges now. Celebrate successes, acknowledge the hard work you have put into improving your teaching practice, and set new goals. This can even become another journal entry!

Chapter 6

Making the Most of Learning Opportunities

December

1

Thursday

The Cricket

What did I observe about the children?

Today a little joy hopped into our classroom — a cricket! Following that event, I was reminded how much the children can gain from following their curiosity. At the time we noticed the cricket, a number of the children were manipulating the large, hollow blocks in the block area, and Mason, Kyra, and Liam had begun to build. Meanwhile, Clyde, Declan, and Avery had started to explore some house-area materials that would extend their play. They decided they needed glasses, gloves, and orange vests to carry out their plan.

As Mason and Liam began to grab more blocks, the secret-agent play moved back into the block area, and Clyde noticed something out of the corner of his eye. "Hey…" he said, with a note of wonder and curiosity, "I saw something over there. A bug I think!" Curious myself, I began to help the children rearrange the blocks so we could see what it might be. As we carefully lifted each block, the children moved closer and closer; some of the "secret agents" approached the scene as well. And then, when I lifted an-other block — "There!" said Mason, who was watching intently. The children started to shriek in delight as they saw the cricket moving around. I said, "You're excited about this cricket. I'm worried we might scare him away, though. I wonder if we could spy on him and give him some space so that he doesn't get scared." At that point, Clyde was already on his hands and knees — "I'm going to use my flashlight," he said.

Children use binoculars and flashlights to catch a better glimpse of a cricket that found its way into the classroom.

Before I knew it, six of the children were huddled around the hollow blocks, watching the moving cricket from multiple angles. As we observed (aided by flashlights, glasses, binoculars, and the proper apparel — gloves and vests, of course!), we shared a rich conversation about this creature that had halted our play and yet was sustaining it at the same time. Then, as the cricket stilled, the children grew quiet and just watched. After a few moments, as the cricket began to move again, the children followed it around and commented

The children's interest was sustained as they wondered aloud together what the cricket would do next.

on what it was doing — what its movements were like, in which direction it was moving, and what it looked like. The children asked questions and wondered aloud together, with questions such as "Where did it come from?"; "Was it hungry?"; "Why did it stop?"; "Is it still scared?"; and "Does it like the light?"

After a bit, the cricket began hopping around more. As its activity increased, some of the children shied away, but Clyde became all the more intrigued. He scooped up the cricket and began to examine it up close. As the other children's curiosity began to wane, I spoke to Clyde about where he thought the cricket might live and what it might need to survive. We agreed that the cricket needed to go back outside, where it had come from, so a few of the children followed me to the door, and we let the cricket go and watched it hop away.

Providing Simple Choices for Everyday Tasks

Building on what I already know

As I continue to reflect on HighScope's approach, new ideas come forward and old ideas shift in my mind. My understanding of the curriculum and its application continues to grow the more I learn, observe, and practice. Early on in my training, I learned about the five ingredients of active learning — one of which is choice. When I first started thinking about active learning, I expected choice-making mainly in the following parts of the daily routine:

- **Plan-do-review and outside time:** Children choose what they want to do at work time — how they want the activity to play out, who they will work with, where they'll work, and which materials they'll use. They also choose what to share at planning and recall times and how they may want to use props when planning or recalling.

- **Large-group time:** Children choose how to move their bodies and how to use materials.

- **Small-group time:** Children choose how to use the materials given for the activity, and they choose who they might like to collaborate with.

- **Snacktime:** Children choose what to eat, what to drink, and which snacktime job to sign up for.

In general, I was associating choice with materials, use of materials, work-time scenarios, and play partnerships. As the year has progressed, however, I have come to see just how helpful giving children choices can be as a strategy for problem prevention. For example, choices help kids with transitions and otherwise potentially difficult times in the day. Offering choices to children empowers them, making them feel they have some control over their day. I had been giving children choices throughout the entire day, but until recently I hadn't fully realized their potential effects and benefits. Here are some times of day that I had initially overlooked when thinking about this component of active learning:

- **Greeting time:** Settling in for the morning is an important transition. We always congregate on the large rug for greeting time. The children hang up their things and sign in — then they know they can sit down on the carpet with one of the two choices available to them: books or a simple material (such as chalkboards, whiteboards, or magnetic boards with letters or other magnets) that they can explore while sitting on the floor. There is a subtle but meaningful difference between telling a child to choose a book and allowing the child to choose between finding a book and sitting down with just one other alternative material. *Examples of what we say:* "You can choose to read a book or write on the dry-erase boards." "Would you like to use the magnetic letters or read a story?"

- **Transitions:** Asking the children how they would like to move to the next part of the day also involves them in the process of transitioning. *Examples of what we say:* "How would you like to move to small-group time? Do you want to try what Mason is doing? He's jumping to small-group time." Also, I'll often start singing a song (especially while beginning snacktime) and let the children fill in part of the verse. For example, "Willaby, Wallaby, Wide, a _____ sat on Clyde…."

- **Cleanup:** Using a variety of engaging whole-group cleanup strategies is important, but supporting children on an individual level is important as well. Giving children choices about how or what to put away makes the process more collaborative and productive. *Examples of what we say:* "Would you like to pick up the cars or the blocks?"; "How would you like to carry the blocks?"; "Are you choosing to start cleaning up in the house area or the book area?"

- **End of the day:** Sometimes parents arrive late to pick up their children. Transitioning from outside time (which occurs at the end of our day) to going back indoors, where we wait for parents or other family members who are late, can be quite a difficult transition. But making it fun and giving children choices helps this process. *Examples of what we say:* "Would you like to hop back into the classroom or run into the classroom?"; "How would you like to move your body to the gate?"; "When you're inside, you can choose a book or a puzzle."

15
Thursday

Creating Materials to Solve Problems and Enhance Pretend Play

What did I observe about the children?

Sometimes visitors to the HighScope Demonstration Preschool will ask "How do you help children problem-solve when they just don't want to compromise?" We use a number of strategies while following the six steps of conflict resolution (see sidebar on p. 5). When a toy or other material is in dispute, we guide children through the conflict resolution steps and listen to their ideas. Sometimes a child or teacher may suggest that one of the children use an alternative toy or material, rather than the object in question. We have found that at times this may mean encouraging the child to make something new to replace the material that the two children each want.

Related to the last point is something that has come from Shannon's and my continued self-questioning: "How can we extend superhero, princess, or other pretend play that has become somewhat flat?" I have found that the children are able to pursue their interests a bit further, supplementing their pretend play, by making props or costumes to pair with their role-playing ideas. Thus, creating something to support play can complement both pretending and problem solving.

Building on what I already know

This week a number of children have been very engaged in making things, mainly in the art area. The following gives an example of how creating materials from other materials was part of problem solving.

Yesterday, Kyra and Nikki were arguing about "the purple dress." This dress has become a coveted item in our house area clothes rack, and both girls wanted to use it at the same time. The dress (full-length on a preschooler) is made of purple and black velour fabric. I approached the girls calmly while holding the dress, and proceeded to acknowledge each girl's feelings as we talked about the problem. However, even after much acknowledgement of their feelings, the girls were yelling at each other and expressing angry feelings; they didn't seem ready to provide many ideas about how to solve the problem. Instead, Nikki and Kyra went back and forth for quite awhile, sharply insisting on the first turn with the dress. For example, Kyra said that she wanted the dress today and Nikki could have it tomorrow — to which Nikki replied with a firm "No!" A couple of children looked on at different points in the process, and I tried to refer Nikki and Kyra to their peers. "Maybe Mina has an idea," I said at one point. Mina said she thought one of them could use the blue dress, and Clyde suggested that they use the sand timer to take turns; but the girls didn't like either of these choices.

After a while I shared my thoughts with the girls — I told them I was worried that they would run out of time to carry out their work-time plans because we were still focusing on the problem. I asked them if they would like to hear my idea, and they both said "yes." "I wonder if you could *make* something to wear," I prompted. Kyra looked over to the art area and exclaimed, "Hey I can make a dress!" Before I knew it, Kyra had thrown the purple dress to Nikki and moved on to find materials with which to create her new dress.

I help Kyra attach the dress she created during work time.

She grabbed some foil and started to think about how she could attach it to her body. At the same time, I wondered aloud if she wanted the dress to be a certain color. "Well, maybe I could make it purple," she said. So Kyra grabbed a marker and began to color the foil. After she had colored a piece and held it up to her body, she realized that she would need more foil, so she taped another piece of foil and colored that in too. She followed this process once more, and then asked me to help her put on the dress. I held the foil pieces up to Kyra in various ways as we tried to plan a way to lay out and attach them to her clothes. Kyra decided that the parts with the most purple needed to be in front. She cut the tape and I held the "fabric" as she told me where to affix each piece of tape. When we were done, Kyra looked down at herself and began to jump up and down excitedly. "I need a crown!" she shouted, and went over to get some paper to work on a crown.

What went well?

Observing children creating something to use in their play allows us to really appreciate the benefits of open-ended materials in the classroom. Today, Declan was very engaged in reading a book about bones that a staff member had donated. He was fascinated with a page illustrating a snake skeleton — so much so that he made a plan to be a snake during work time. He starting slithering around on the carpet but wasn't quite sure what to do next. I talked with him about what snakes do, what they eat, where they live, and what they look like. When Declan referred back to the book, he started talking to me more about the features of the snake and the shapes and orientation of its bones. When I reminded Declan about the mask he had made on a previous day of school, he asked me if he could make a snake mask. Declan then became very involved in selecting the materials to make his snake mask and referring back to the original resource — the donated book about bones — to discover how he could draw the shape he needed for his mask. He then cut out and wore his creation.

Declan uses a nonfiction book as a resource for pretend play. Referencing a snake's skeleton, Declan draws and cuts out a snake form, which he will wear during work time.

Problem Solving and Mathematics

Building on what I already know

Veronica, Mina, and the blocks. Today, Veronica arrived at the block area first and began building. Then Mina arrived and started to build too. Mina approached Veronica to talk to her about the blocks; Veronica wanted to use all of the blocks. "There's lots of shelves, Veronica," Mina said, referring to the layers of large blocks stacked against the wall. "Well, I need them," replied Veronica insistently. This is when I stepped in to guide the girls through problem solving.

As I first started thinking about what was going on, I realized that the girls' problem solving really built on the use of math concepts. For starters, the premise of the problem revolved around the following concepts, which both girls understood:

- *Size:* Both children needed big blocks to make big castles.

- *Amount:* They both needed many blocks to make big castles.

When I wondered aloud with the girls about how we might solve the problem, Mina said she needed some blocks but that Veronica didn't want to give any up. I asked the girls if they wanted to hear my idea, and they said they did. As the blocks were split into what looked like two nearly equal amounts, I pointed to one pile and said, "I wonder if one of you could use this pile…" then I pointed to the other pile and said, "…and one of you could use this pile." Veronica still didn't want to share. At that point, Mina started counting, saying "This one has 1, 2, 3, 4, 5, 6, 7, 8, 9, 10, 11, 12 — 12." Then she counted the blocks near Veronica from 1 to 14. She said, "You have more, Veronica." Veronica, finally giving in, said, "You can use some of these. They will fit in those parts," and she showed Mina where some of her smaller blocks would fit into the pile Mina had begun.

Through the six steps of problem solving, the children explored math concepts, including size, number, more than/less than, space/geometry (fitting smaller pieces into smaller spaces), and comparison.

The large, hollow, wooden blocks are a classroom favorite that provide both opportunities for problem solving and for exploring many math concepts.

Follow-Up to "Problem Solving and Mathematics"

Ideas and insights

Today I made an effort to look for similar math-related problem-solving opportunities throughout the daily routine. I thought that if I knew more about how the children were naturally exploring such concepts, perhaps I could better meet their needs by scaffolding a variety of math experiences throughout the day. As it turned out, a situation similar to the one involving Mina and Veronica yesterday arose today between Declan and Mina. Declan and Mina were using the large blocks. Declan was upset because he only had four blocks.

Mina said, "Four is a lot." Declan replied by saying, "No, four is a little 'cause one, two, three, four." Mina responded by telling Declan that he had counted too fast. "Five is big," Declan said, and Mina agreed. Then she counted blocks from one to six. "Whoa," said Declan, smiling, "That's a lot." Mina then gave Declan two blocks so he had six — the number he agreed was a lot.

After this conversation, Declan chose to move on to another activity, pleased with the different but perfectly acceptable turn of events in the block area. Both of the children were satisfied with where their exploration had taken them, and Mina continued to build.

Later, at the sand and water table, Kyra and Clyde were trying to solve a problem with the "cloud dough" (a powdery substance made of baby oil and flour), and I observed them and some other children problem solving by using math concepts. Earlier during work time, some children had moved most of the dough from one side of the table to the other. When Kyra came to the table, most of the dough was on Clyde's side, and he was scooping it into a large bin. He stirred his recipe.

Kyra announced. "Look right here, Becky. I have less." Clyde said, "Well I need more because I'm making stuff." Miriam popped over at this time and said, "Well, there's lots over here and right here," pointing to where the cloud dough had collected along the inside edge of the table bins. "I know!" said Kyra. "I'll scoop it up!"

This child uses math skills as he judges how many balls will fit in the basket.

At the end of work time, I also observed ways in which math concepts were woven into cleanup time. The children talked about how many things they could put away, compared amounts, and used the concepts of one-to-one correspondence, patterning, and spatial awareness to put things in their places.

As I walked over to help the children in the book area, Finn said, "Too many," referring to the woven balls scattered around the area. "I can put three," Nikki said. "I can hold more," said Clyde, taking them from his shirt and plopping them into the basket where we store them. Finn collected one at a time, and they accomplished the task together.

What I Learned This Month

Here are some conclusions I've drawn from my own active learning experiences this month:

- Children direct the play in HighScope classrooms, but teachers still set the stage. In other words, children look to teachers when questions arise or when they are wondering how to respond to something new. This is important to remember when odd things happen and one finds a cricket hiding behind a block! Teachers have the power to either become directive and stomp out learning or to join in the children's excitement and scaffold the active learning that has the potential to unfold.

- Offering children choices empowers children. Children grow in their sense of competence and responsibility as they make meaningful choices about how the next important step in their day will pan out. Children learn to collaborate with adults and other children instead of just abiding by rules that are given to them. In short, they are active participants in their learning and in daily choices that affect their lives.

- Open-ended materials in the classroom provide ample opportunities for the children to create new materials with which to solve problems and develop their play.

- Math is everywhere in the preschool classroom! If we intentionally support language that incorporates mathematics, we will soon find children comparing, counting, and sorting during play, conversation, and problem solving throughout the daily routine.

Chapter 7

Fresh Inspiration

January

12

Thursday

New Students and New Materials

Ideas and insights

I absolutely cannot believe it is January. Do we say this every year? Every month? This new year brought two more students into our classroom. We welcomed Jason and Fatima, both three years old, and as we did so, we became even more excited about the semester ahead. We placed Jason in Shannon's group, thinking he'd work well with Liam and Finn, two other three-year-olds. We placed Fatima in my group, having noticed from her prior visit that she and Nikki seemed instantly to have a good connection.

Building on what I already know

We decided to make some other changes as well. We altered the makeup of the learning environment for the second semester by adding a woodworking table to the art area (along with real hammers, nails, screws, and screwdrivers to start) and putting computers in the book area. Each year we wait to add these materials to the learning environment in order to allow the younger children to progress in using some of the simpler open-ended materials. This allows them to become familiar with the areas by using a less complex clustering of manipulatives, tools, and other materials.

We want to give the children practical and guided experiences with the woodworking tools, most often through small-group experiences at first, where it is most possible to scaffold each child's learning. Usually this means beginning with painting, coloring, or gluing wood and Styrofoam. We then progress to pressing golf tees into Styrofoam, then to using hammers and nails, then to using screws, and eventually to having experiences with hand drills. Levels, measuring tapes, and other tools can also be included along the way. The children always wear safety glasses to protect their eyes in the woodworking area. Once we bring out the woodworking table, we focus on supporting and expanding children's play in appropriate and safe ways (including keeping the woodworking area materials at the woodworking table). Last year we had

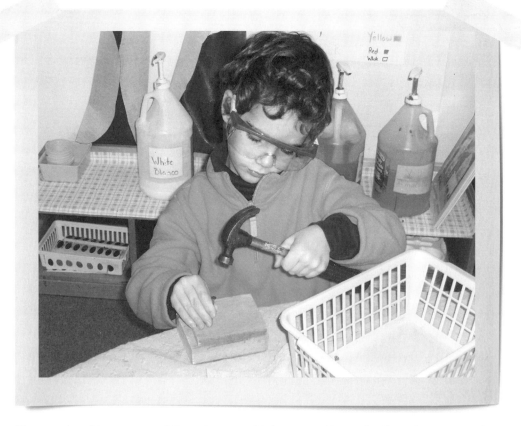

The woodworking area and the art area, which are next to each other, share a number of materials.

the woodworking table in its own area. This year we thought that the space available near the art area lent itself well to the woodworking table, and that placing the woodworking table there would be a minor change that would not disturb the children.

What went well?

We introduced children to the computers in the book area through simple, open-ended learning activities. In general, we encourage the children — especially those who seem to gravitate toward such technology — to balance their time on the computer during work time with time spent using other materials. For example, Clyde absolutely loves spending time on the computer. As this is his second year at the Demonstration Preschool, Clyde remembers that he will spend only part of his work time on the computer before moving on to something else. I remind him of this expectation immediately during planning time. That is, when Clyde plans to go to the book area and play on the computer, I prompt him by saying "I wonder what your second plan will be." This way, he already has an idea for what to do after computer time.

Clyde has grown comfortable with tools that help him manage his time while using the computer; namely, a sand timer and a sign-up sheet. This sign-up sheet is specifically for the use of the computers. It is a simple sheet that says "Computers" at the top, with lines underneath. The children practice writing their names to hold their place for using a computer, and we work on taking turns together. However, most of the learning at the computers takes place when a number of children gather around one computer and share that experience and language together.

Both the sign-up sheet and sand timer help Clyde (and other children) understand when the next waiting child will begin his or her turn at the computer. The children don't yet know how to tell time, but they use the sand timers to help them visualize the passing of time. They know they have choices, and they will say things like "I'm going to use the big sand timer" (or the medium sand timer). This is another reason I find it beneficial to wait until the second semester to bring out the computers. At that point in the year, the children are more comfortable with all the learning areas and the materials and choices available to them. They are also more familiar with the concept of sign-in/sign-up sheets (which we use at greeting time and snacktime as well), our problem solving process, and the uses and benefits of sand timers, and they are also better able to engage in more than one plan.

In our classroom, we have sand timers of various sizes made from empty plastic bottles.

Large-Group Stretches

Ideas and insights

When I first started my teaching career, I was finishing my undergraduate degree and substitute teaching on the side. I was always pressed for time, and at the end of the day, I needed a way to wind down. Each evening, I began using basic stretching to help me get centered and ready to transition to the next part of my day, whether it was cooking, reading, or painting. Introducing our preschool children to simple stretches is something that I have been wanting to do during large-group time for quite a while. However, I've also wanted to make sure that I introduce it in a way that makes sense to the children. Because so much of our daily routine incorporates simple symbols and stick figures, I decided to use these kinds of graphic representations to help the children visualize what the stretches would look like. Using fun names and making sounds and movements that relate the stretches to animals or other natural objects is a great way to incorporate pretending into this gross-motor activity (for example, meowing like a cat while arching our backs or standing straight and swaying gently from side to side like a tree). I spoke with my fitness instructor, Malissa, to get some ideas for what the pictures (and the fun names) could be (e.g., "stretching as tall as a *tree*"). This was particularly helpful so I could follow the same, simple, universal stick figure forms that we use on our message board. You can see the cards that I created on page 120.

What went well?

I introduced the large-group time activity by talking about what fitness classes are like and about how deep breathing when stretching helps to get oxygen into the body. I also showed the children a few of the basic stretches on cards. We talked about how we slow down when we stretch, and we described the shapes our bodies were making.

What did I observe about the children?

It was interesting to watch the children as they read the cards and interpreted each in their own way. Some of the children chose to imitate the shape of the stick figure, and some chose a little variation. We will continue to try stretching at large-group time, and plan to progress from using simple stretches in isolation to those which are a bit more complex or done in sequence. We expect the children to invent some new stretches of their own, which we will add to our repertoire. We might stretch to music or use stretches as a warmup to another large-group activity.

Very often, large-group time is a part of the daily routine when children explore moving their bodies or other materials using fast movements. Engaging in stretching lets kids try out something new at a slower pace while exploring balance. We talk about our bodies, about calming down, and about healthy behaviors related to our stretching and movement.

The children stretch like a star, while I hold the stick-figure stretch card.

A child stretches and curves her back.

Becky's Group: Recall Time

What support do I need?

I continue to struggle with my group at recall time particularly.

Supporting children in their groups. We have tried to create groups of children that reflect a variety of developmental levels, backgrounds, and personalities, in order to enrich children's experience at recall time as well as the other times they meet in their small groups. We want the children to work well together so they can learn from and support one another as they manipulate materials, express themselves, collaborate, and explore new challenges. It has been difficult to maintain consistent groups because we have a smaller number of children in the program this year; in addition, with fewer children in each group, the range of interests and developmental levels is more limited. I continue to feel hesitations about changing the makeup of groups as much as we have, but when we have done so, it has been to facilitate the best learning experiences for the children. Determining the makeup of each group is a complex process — one that usually begins with one part insight and two parts trial and error. Again, the goal is for the groups to remain as consistent as possible. But sometimes we decide it is more important to pair or separate certain children as a way to support their social relationships and other learning.

Supporting children individually. While recall time is still effective, I feel that something has been missing. For the class, it is the group aspects of the process that haven't seemed to gel. I do know that the children are grasping the concept of recall to a certain extent. They are able to verbally, concretely, and even abstractly demonstrate what they did during work time. But what I am struggling with is that this happens mostly at the individual level. I know that the children are having positive recall-time experiences, but I do not see the same level of collaborative recalls within the group that I saw last year. Here's an example of what I mean by "collaborative": if one child recalls building a castle, another might say, "Yeah, I was there, and I cooked with her. We made pizza!" And a third child might say, "And I was the dog, but then I went to the sand and water table."

Fresh Inspiration

Am I having these concerns because I'm expecting to see what I observed when last year's children recalled in the final months of the school year? I'm not sure. But when I look over at Shannon's table, it seems that their recalls are slightly more cohesive. The children are generally paying attention to one another's recalls (as much as can be expected, of course), and they are also supporting one another by jumping in with a description of what they did with or near another child. What happens at my table has been more scattered, and I sometimes feel pulled in various directions — one child here may be wandering off, two children there may be yelling at one another and laughing about it, and another child might be attempting to climb onto the table — all while yet another child starts to recall.

Not every time of the day is like this. When we are at the table for small-group time or for planning time, the children are more engaged. Certainly that could have something to do with the materials they are using, but I think that the fact that they finish their work-time activities at various times affects their

At recall time, children take turns talking about what they did at work time.

engagement with recall, which we strive to make a group process. In considering this, I sometimes wonder if I should be allowing more opportunities for children to leave recall as needed. (Sometimes I do ask the children to leave the table one at a time to begin washing their hands for snack.)

I also know that not everyone needs to recall every day, but I haven't really been practicing this — I still ask each of the children to recall. In addition, I want the children to be able to support one another's recalls. I think what it comes down to is my struggle to maintain the children's attention and keep them engaged, yet not *pulling* them in and directing them to pay attention. I am not expecting the children to "sit still," but I often find myself perplexed because I sometimes want to say, "stop talking" or "listen to Fatima's recall." I am keenly aware that if I were to give in to these thoughts, I would run the risk of being too directive, but I am also concerned that recall is less meaningful without as many children lending their attention and ideas to the process.

What did I notice about the children?

Reflecting on children's learning through my writing is definitely helping me to sort through the real issues. Here are some undeniable truths:

1. Recall time is not engaging the whole group.

2. Miriam and Clyde are very silly together, and it's distracting for themselves and others.

3. Fatima is new, still learning, and perhaps even testing me.

4. Mason is a keen observer — to the extent that he is constantly jumping out of his seat to move the daily routine clip to the next segment of the day, to see what Shannon's group is up to, or to put away a block that he has seen is out of place from the corner of his eye. How can I engage him to use his interest in the connections between things in a positive way?

5. I have tried a variety of recall strategies, and I know that some strategies work better than others. I'm not sure whether the problems I've seen with recall relate to the types of strategies I've used. Perhaps using more group-focused recall strategies would provide the most benefit.

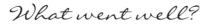

What went well?

I feel that I am working effectively with these situations. I continue to redirect Mason, and I appreciate his genuine interest in everything that's happening — it does not have to take away from the group; rather it can add to it tremendously. Additionally, as Fatima is new to our classroom, I have been rather focused on guiding her through the day. To help her integrate into the learning environment and the group of children, I use sign language, labels, and daily routine pictures as well as reminders and referrals to other children. I feel sure that these strategies will also end up having a positive effect on recall time.

Follow-up

We decided to move Miriam to Shannon's group, and it has really helped both Clyde and Miriam become more independent as they make choices about their day. Clyde and Miriam still check in with one another to plan, and they often choose to play together, but they are both more engaged during table times: planning time, recall time, snacktime, and small-group time.

Shannon noticed that one reason the children at my table had been distracted was that they had wanted to move the clip on the daily routine chart. (Since the transitions from cleanup to recall and from recall to snacktime happen quickly, the children are very aware of them, and this may make them think of moving the clip.) We talked to the children at my table about this (my group is closest to the daily routine chart, and therefore more inclined to want to monitor it at table times) and told them that moving the clip could be done *during* transitions. This has helped to keep them more focused at the table.

Recall revisited. I've also tried to plan more intentionally around the goal of children recalling *as a group,* that is, as a small community of learners. After consulting some resources, including the HighScope book *Making the Most of Plan-Do-Review* by Nancy Vogel, I made a list of recall strategies to try that are more conducive to whole-group engagement. Here they are:

- *Mystery bag:* The teacher places in the bag materials that the children have used (for example, a Duplo, a dinosaur figure, a paintbrush, etc.). Then the teacher or a child (or children taking turns) pulls one item out at a time. Because each child has one or more materials he or she played with in the bag, each child eagerly waits and watches to see what comes out next. Then they all comment on who they remember playing with each material that is pulled out of the bag. This helps a conversation about what happened around that material begin to unfold.

- *Hula Hoop:* Children sit in a circle with the teacher, and everyone holds on to the Hula Hoop. The Hula Hoop is marked by a piece of masking tape on one place. The group chooses a song to sing and rotates the hoop through everyone's hands as they sing. As the hoop is passed along, the piece of tape moves from child to child. When the song ends, the child whose hand is on the tape gets to recall (this game is much like "hot potato"). Because the children are seated closely together, the setting helps bring the children into recall conversations.

- *Recall storybooks:* One way to do recall storybooks is to include a different child's recall on each page. Another option is a more group-focused storybook, organized around what happened in each area, with one area's activities described per page. In this way, if one child says, "I used the measuring cups in the sand and water table," another child can add, "Yeah, me too! I did that with him, but I was using the shovels."

What I Learned This Month

Here are some conclusions I've drawn from my own active learning experiences this month:

- Bringing in new materials and rearranging the classroom a bit after a break in the school year can bring a welcome sense of renewal to the classroom community. As with all of the choices we make in our role as teachers, we can intentionally plan to offer materials and create a learning environment that will support children and foster their learning in new and meaningful ways. Adding an entirely new area (in our case, the woodworking area), can also bring excitement in a way that is nonthreatening to the children's expectations for their environment — that is, if children's development, interests, and needs are carefully considered in making such changes.

- Offering simple, yet engaging physical education practices during large-group time, such as the stretching exercises we did, has given me a chance to share my excitement and passion for these activities. Moreover, using simple visual cues and props can help children learn and explore new ways to move their bodies during large-group time, just as they do throughout other parts of the daily routine.

- Recall time is a very important part of our preschool day. During this time, children and adults share their work-time experiences and reflect on what was created, experienced, said, and understood during work time. Communication that is rich in vocabulary is shared during recall as children reflect on what they did and what they remember others doing. Children and adults can then use this information to form ideas about how successes and challenges came about and were handled, and what they might choose to do in the future. Recall time can be challenging, but there are many strategies teachers can use to make recall time successful and enriching for all.

Chapter 8

Learning and Practicing

February

1

Wednesday

Involving Families

Building on what I already know

We had a visitor at the Demonstration Preschool yesterday, and her comments got me thinking. She was so thrilled to see all the little ways in which parents are involved in their children's morning here. At first I didn't think much of it, but when she came back to visit again today, and continued to commend our parents, I couldn't help but take a step back and think about it myself. As I write this, I'm noting that, while I usually refer to children's parents, guardians, or caregivers as *families,* this year all of our children are living with their moms and/or dads. However, we also have a number of grandparents, aunts, and uncles who come to pick up the children at the end of the day.

Although parents helped lead both small groups yesterday (Jason's parents explored flour and water with the children as they showed the children how Chinese dumplings are made — one parent worked with each small group), our visitor was more interested in the everyday ways in which our parents participate in the day. When children arrive for the morning and when they leave at the end of the day, of course family members are there. I suppose this is true in many programs, although I know that the truth is that sometimes children are quickly dropped off and collected, without a longer and more meaningful transition, and some children are bussed.

When I think about how parents interact with the children in our classroom, I am proud. The parents help lead their children into the daily routine each day with love and care. Sure, some families carpool, and some parents need to get to work after a moment or so at dropoff time; but in general, the atmosphere in the morning provides a comfortable transition for children into the school day. I had never really considered this until now, but I think it is our routine that allows for this consistent togetherness. Book reading at greeting time provides such a beautiful opportunity for adults and children to bond, but these other parts of our early morning also specifically help connect families to our program:

- **Sign-in:** Family members walk their child into the classroom and greet teachers and the other children. They ease the transition into the school day by supporting their child as the child hangs up his or her coat and writes his or her name on the sign-in sheet.

- **Greeting time:** Often, parents will stay through our time at the message board, which is at the end of greeting time, sharing this experience with their preschooler (and sometimes their preschooler's younger sibling). This year, we have been transitioning from greeting time into planning time (and occasionally a parent will stay to help his or her child plan); but last year, large-group time followed greeting time. Parents would often stay and move or sing with their children. It was wonderful!

- **Outside time:** Outside time takes place during the last half-hour of our morning program, right after small-group time. A number of families arrive early for pickup so they can spend time on the playground with their child and his or her younger siblings. Some adult family members often arrive early enough to help with small-group cleanup and interact with the children as they do so. One mother has even been taking it upon herself to help clean up the classroom while we're out on the playground. There is a real sense of community when everyone is working together in this way. Parents also use this time to mingle, share, and plan play dates together.

This child and her father look through a class collection of family photos during greet-ing time.

There are additional opportunities for families to spend time with teach-ers and other families in the classroom community, such as the following:

* **Home visits twice per year.** This is an opportunity for families and teachers to get acquainted, for teachers to see children in their home

environment, and for teachers to give parents information about active learning in the home.

- **Visits to our classroom.** This year, in addition to Jason's parents showing the children how to make Chinese dumplings at small-group time, one father who is a musician brought in his band for large-group time. Another dad, who drives the local library's bookmobile, came one day to share books with the children.

- **Field trips.** These also include walking trips around our campus and downtown community.

- **Donating to the classroom.** We encourage families to bring in house-area materials; the children enjoy choosing empty food containers from their home kitchens to bring into our classroom. Families also share photographs, which we add to classroom books and to displays.

- **Parent nights.** These events give us an opportunity to introduce more of the curriculum to the families, as well as to explore specific parenting issues of interest and importance to parents. At these meetings, we discuss the HighScope Curriculum and share strategies from the classroom, and we also refer parents to one another. The parents are definitely able to relate to one another as caretakers of young children. It is so inspiring to share information with family members and see them making connections with one another and exchanging ideas.

We also use the following events and strategies to involve parents at our preschool, in addition to our parent-teacher conferences.

- **Potlucks.** We tend to have at least three potlucks per year — in September, December, and June.

- **Playground workdays.** We have asked for family volunteers to help us with some playground update projects that we received grant funding for. We hope to have work days like these every year.

- **Observations.** We have groups of visitors in our Demonstration Preschool about twice a month. We reserve one visit for our preschool families to watch our daily routine in action.

- **Family visits.** Families are also welcome in the classroom during any part of the daily routine. Once in a while, parents choose to stick around and be with their child during work time or other times of the day.

Parents and a teacher work together to move and refurbish the existing playground sandbox.

- **Forms of communication.** E-mail has been a huge help this year, especially with a gentle push from Jason's family. He and his parents are here from China, and after we began e-mailing families, Jason's parents replied to all with an invitation for play dates. Jason arrived at a time when Fatima was new to our classroom too (mid school year) so it was also a real help to her family to be welcomed in this way.

- **Calendars.** We make calendars listing special events taking place in the classroom that also include ideas for family interactions printed on them that family members can take home (see the sample on p. 134).

- **Literacy activity bags.** This is a simple activity that connects to a children's book we provide. Each bag includes a copy of the book, a related material, and an instruction card for how to implement and extend the activity while supporting language development with a child. These also help add to the home-school connection.

October

HighScope Demonstration Preschool

Sunday	Monday	Tuesday	Wednesday	Thursday	Friday	Saturday
						1
2	3 Wasem's apple orchard field trip.	4	5	6 PAJAMA DAY! Wear PJ's to celebrate Jumpstart Reading Program and the Llama, Llama, Red Pajama book.	7	8 Work on your family photo page together if you haven't already.
9	10	11 Work on a puzzle together.	12	13	14	15 Visit the library.
16 Do something outside.	17	18 PARENT MEETING, 6-7 PM Topic: Active learning.	19	20 Find some empty food containers that you wish to add to the house area!	21	22
23	24	25 Ask your child to help set the table.	26	27	28	29
30	31 Halloween: Bring your costume to school!					

February

9

Thursday

Work-Time Focus

What didn't go as I had planned?

Lately I have really been feeling guilty at work time. It seems that no matter what I intend to do, I'm being pulled in a number of other directions. I feel that I've been able to meet children's needs and appropriately scaffold their development, yet I'm not able to give them all the attention they desire. I want to be able to spend quality time engaging with individual children in their play, but when I do that, I find I'm also needed by other children. Sometimes, it unfolds like this: a child wants my attention or would like to assign me a role in his or her pretend play. At that very moment, I also see another child wandering the room who is in need of some support to replan, or who needs help problem solving. Even though Shannon and I are constantly juggling, I don't always feel this imbalance, so this shift in how I'm feeling has led me to wonder what I can do to better meet children's needs.

As a teacher, I am used to multitasking! I want to support my students through scaffolding, and some children need more or different help from Shannon and me than do others, depending on what they plan. During work time, I am mindful of my interactions with children as they seek or need attention and support.

I know that the children are capable of accomplishing many things independently and/or together with their peers. (I also understand that I need to always have my attention on the whole room to some degree, in case a child needs immediate assistance). However, I also know how beneficial it is to truly engage and commit to play scenarios alongside the children.

Building on what I already know

One thing that helps me be intentional in my teaching at work time is to plan a teaching focus on our teachers' daily planning sheet. Sometimes our goal is broad, and sometimes it is more specific, but it always stems from what we've observed during recent work times and/or how we expect the children to work.

I talk with a child about her play.

For example, yesterday (when planning for today) Shannon and I planned to support children's sand and water table activity today because we recently added many tubes and pipes to the area, and we expected that it would be a "high traffic" area in the classroom today. Last week, we planned to support superhero play because so many kids were engaging in this type of play but were getting "stuck" about how to proceed after only a few minutes of work time. Other plans have included supporting one specific child to be engaged, helping children replan, and supporting problem solving (or more specifically, focusing on one step in resolving conflicts, such as acknowledging feelings).

What support do I need?

I talked to Shannon after school about feeling pulled in many directions at work time. She said that, in some ways, she felt the same. She said, "There were so many cool things happening at work time. I wish some of it didn't stop when one of us had to go help another child." She had found, as I had, that when we shift our attention, the engagement of the children we've been focusing on sometimes unravels. Some of the children really yearn for the teacher component of play. Of course, once we are invited into the children's play, we are taking cues from *them* and building upon and supporting their ideas. But sometimes our mere presence helps the younger children, or those at earlier stages of development, engage in parallel play or play more interactively with peers instead of playing independently. Therefore, when we have to step away, these children sometimes lose their focus.

We will continue brainstorming how to best meet the needs of our children at work time. As a start, Shannon's focus is to play with Jason, since he is fairly new to our classroom. My focus is to begin tomorrow's work time with Mina. Mina is an older child in our classroom who has wanted to play with me quite a bit lately. Today it was difficult for me to focus on her pretend play (mermaid-princesses, with me casting spells) when others needed help using the bathroom, cleaning up as we went along, problem solving with others, problem solving with materials, replanning, and troubleshooting with the computer.

February 10 Friday — Follow-Up to "Work-Time Focus"

Ideas and insights

Today I stayed true to my intention to play with Mina first. I approached her and asked if she would like me to be a part of her mermaid-princess play, as I had been yesterday, and I reminded her that I hadn't had much time with her the previous day because I was solving lots of problems. She replied, "Becky, you DID play with me yesterday!" I was glad to hear her say this. She asked me to be the maid in her pretend-play scenario today, and we found a scarf that I could wear around my waist because the apron was already being used. While I played with Mina, she — along with Kyra and Veronica — made a castle out of the large blocks and many materials from the house area. After watching and waiting for an opening in the play, I joined them. Kyra pretended to feed me hot chocolate the moment I arrived at the castle.

Meanwhile, Declan was working on a knight mask in the art area. Shannon had begun helping him, but then she had to go to the house area to help some children problem-solve. Declan pulled me over and showed me what he had started. He needed help cutting out the eye holes he had drawn on the mask with Shannon's help. I got him started cutting and then retreated back to the princess play. But a few minutes later, Declan came back to me, looking quite upset. He had cut clear across the paper by mistake, which left a gaping hole in his mask. I helped him find some more materials, and together we brainstormed how to create the next mask. Then Mina came over and gave me a look. "You have to clean the house with us for the party," she said.

Needless to say, I've been doing a lot of thinking about how to meet the needs of one child and then another child in classroom situations like this. In this instance, with Declan and Mina both wanting my attention and help, I decided to pull both children in and refer them to one another. "Well, Mina," I said, "Maybe you can help us. Declan is getting really frustrated trying to cut this mask. I saw you using the scissors when you made a crown yesterday. Do you think you could help him?" Mina stepped up to the task and showed Declan how to hold the scissors in one hand and turn the paper in the other. Then she said, "Come on, you guys," and the three of us went over to attend the party together.

I have also been thinking about more ways to help children understand what it means when I say something like "I'll be back in just one minute." For example, at outside time when I'm helping a child, I might ask another child to try singing "Twinkle, Twinkle" while he or she waits for me to come and give a push on the swing. (I also refer the children to one another for pushes.) I know the children understand why I am not immediately available when I say something like "There's a problem right now, so I need to stay here while we solve it. I'll come see how it's going with you when I'm finished."

We want to be engaged with all of our children as partners in their play, but there are only two adults in our classroom, so we have to manage within that limitation. Some children need more support to develop their ideas. For example, there are children who plan to be a superhero but spend work time running and wandering around the classroom. We want to engage them in experiences that supplement their activity of choice, such as by helping them to explore many facets of their role playing. Declan was making a mask because we had helped him to think about what a knight looks like and what a knight does. The girls were building a castle and cooking because they extended their pretend play to include where princesses live, what they eat, and so forth. In my work with most of the children, it's all about finding that balance between being there to help them develop their ideas through meaningful adult-child interactions and allowing them to solve problems on their own or collaboratively with peers.

Large-Group Time

What went well?

Today we sang "Goin' on a Bear Hunt" for our main large-group activity. This time we built on children's previous experience by giving them rhythm sticks to keep a steady beat. We had also sung this song yesterday (after having read the book countless times during greeting time and snacktime), and today the children remembered the tune. Having something in their hands also was useful in helping children stay focused.

What did I observe about the children?

Our easy-to-join activity today was a simple "watch and copy" (this is when we demonstrate a movement and ask children simply to watch, then have children copy the movement as we do it again).

Shannon began the activity by asking a few of the children who were already on the carpet where we gather for large-group time (others were still finishing snack and snack cleanup) if they had ever heard of a mime. She explained that a mime only uses body movements (not voice) to show someone what he or she means. The children copied Shannon after she demonstrated each of several movements. As more and more children joined the group, Shannon progressed from one movement to two-movement patterns, then to four different movements (tap head, then waist, then knees, then toes).

Jason, who is new to our class, was running around the carpet and screaming. He was very excited to be with the other children in this whole-group setting. I have observed that he enjoys moving his body, trying new

things, experimenting with his voice, and just generally being silly. He has fun!
But during the easy-to-join activity, Jason's actions made it difficult for other
kids to follow the leader. One child at a time had been coming up with ideas
for movement patterns to follow, but soon a number of the children began
watching Jason instead of the leading child. I approached Jason and softly
took his hands while explaining to him that it was Kyra's turn to choose how
to move. With my hands gently over his, I copied Kyra's movements so that he
could feel what we were doing. After a few rounds, Jason continued copying
the leader on his own and was later able to take a turn leading the group.

Ideas and insights

We have been concentrating on making large-group time more engaging for the
children. I think that sometimes keeping children's attention at large group has
been a struggle because this time period is sometimes longer than necessary.
Recently we've also tried these strategies: doing new or less-frequently-used
activities; using the class song book less often (we had been using it regularly)

Children and teachers work together in an easy-to-join activity.

and changing the songs included in the song book; using carpet squares to help give the children a sense of their own personal body space; and introducing a social story (see pp. 9–10 for more on social stories). Our hope is that using these strategies will help children understand some of the distractions we've seen happening at large-group time and to help brainstorm possible solutions. Using social stories helps us find ideas for solutions as well.

I think as we continue to grow as a classroom community this year, it's important for us to use a variety of materials, songs, movements, and activities for large-group experiences. We started a list of class favorites so we can keep better track of which activities we have done recently. Shannon and I also plan to keep our focus on the purpose of the easy-to-join activities — *to allow kids to transition to large-group time by keeping things simple at the start.* With this in mind, we'll try not to let the opening activity become more involved than we had intended.

February

20

Monday

Clyde's Planning

What did I observe about the children?

Over the past two weeks, planning time has been a bit of a struggle for Clyde. His approach to planning time lately has been to repeat the same plan every day: "First I'm going to the computers and then I'm going to 'choo-choo,'" he'll say, prompting me to guess that he'll be working with the trains. When Clyde does this, he is actually sharing *two* plans with me — he is telling me what he plans do first and what he plans to do second. Often, he'll even include more details within these plans — "I'm going to the book area to use computer number one, and then I'm going to the block area to use the trains with Mason." To an outside observer, this would probably seem to be a perfectly acceptable way to plan. What I see as the problem is not in Clyde's planning statement, but rather, in his lack of real intentionality. I've reflected on this quite a bit recently, and I'm not sure whether Clyde is just itching to speed through planning so he can get to work time, or whether he's stuck in one set plan — or perhaps both.

Children plan by "fishing" for the area in which they choose to play during work time.

Before I clarify what I said about Clyde's intentions, it's important to first explain that although Clyde loves to play the computer games, it's not that he is unwilling to do anything else. And he does have an understanding of the concept of "screen time," because his parents limit this at home. Therefore, it is relatively easy to encourage Clyde to move on to a second plan after spending some time on the computer. I do not expect all of the children to tell me about more than one plan, but at this point in the year (and in Clyde's time with us — this is his second year in the classroom), he is very capable of doing this. We have found that guiding Clyde to extend his plan by thinking about what will happen *after* he spends time on the computer helps him to transition from computer games to other materials. I might also mention that Clyde is a very verbal child. He consistently surprises me with his vocabulary and insight. In short, Clyde is fully capable of making and carrying out detailed plans that will result in complex play.

What has been happening lately is that, although Clyde makes a plan to use the computer and then the trains, after he spends time on the computer, he ends up doing something else entirely. I am not concerned about the fact that Clyde engages in other activities, but more that he is not being intentional when he expresses his plans. On most days in the last two weeks, Clyde had planned to use the computers and then the trains, but he never got to the trains. I've been asking myself whether he is interested in the trains but loses interest after his time on the computer and/or whether he simply changes his mind. Or is he just falling back on the train plan during planning time because it's easy for him to repeat from memory? Lately, after Clyde has left the computer area, he has been engaging in pretend play with Miriam, Avery, and Declan (usually role-playing as superheroes or playing "Harry Potter") which sometimes leads to general wandering. He has also been building with large blocks or using the rotators (toys that children sit and spin on) in the block area, has played in the sand and water table, has pretended to be a dog in the house area, and has used the hole-punch with Miriam to make "tickets" for people as they enter various areas.

What support do I need?

I have been reflecting on Clyde's planning with Shannon as we create our daily plans. I have also spoken with Clyde's mom to see if she could shed any light on his planning. I've also been intentionally choosing planning strategies to support Clyde, particularly concrete and engaging strategies that will help him make real choices about his work time. Here are some things I've tried:

At planning time:

- Say to Clyde, "Bring back an object that you'll use." Acknowledge the train as a choice, but ask him to bring back a second choice as well.

- Say to Clyde, "Tell me what you will do after you use the computers."

- Use the train track and train as planning props to help him figure out if these are materials he's actually interested in using, and what he will do with them if he is.

At work time:

- Support and encourage Clyde to transition from the computer to other types of play. Say "How will we know when you're done?"

- Approach Clyde during his play, especially if he seems disengaged. Say "Tell me about your plan."

- If he does move to something else after he finishes with the computers, replan with him: "Clyde, it looks like you have a different plan in mind. Tell me about what you are going to do."

At Recall Time:

- Talk through what happened during work time. Say to Clyde "I noticed that you were going to use the trains, but you changed your plan."

February

21

Tuesday

Follow-Up to "Clyde's Planning"

What did I observe about the children?

Today when Clyde planned with me, it was no different from before. Clyde made a plan to use the computer and then use the train set. I told him what I was thinking: "Clyde, I'm wondering if you really want to use the train. Remember that we talked about how you sometimes plan to use the train, but then you choose to do something else after you finish with the computers." He told me that sometimes he forgets about his train plan, so I suggested that he take the train engine (which he had brought over in a bucket — the planning strategy for today) to the computer and that perhaps that would help him remember.

Ideas and insights

I'm wondering if there is a way to incorporate some of Clyde's other interests into the train play. For example, he likes to act out Thomas the Train's "Misty Island Rescue" movie at the sand and water table. Also, Clyde often chooses the train because he wants to play with Mason — they have developed a close friendship. Maybe I could bring Mason and Clyde together if they are both in transition. I could also encourage Clyde to plan with Mason. The bottom line is that I want Clyde to be engaged during work time. The remaining concern is meaningful planning.

What I Learned This Month

Here are some conclusions I've drawn from my own active learning experiences this month:

- Family involvement is key to establishing a strong classroom community in preschool. But involving families goes much deeper than the occasional family night or parent-teacher conference. In fact, in the Demonstration Preschool classroom, parents and siblings join in classroom experiences, especially while transitioning from home to school (greeting time, story reading, and talking about the message board) and back (supporting children at cleanup and engaging in conversation and play with family members at the end of the school day). Teachers can continue to support such involvement through positive and engaging home-school connection experiences, such as through activity bags and home visits.

- Children and teachers engage in work-time experiences together, as partners in their play. Although it can be difficult for teachers in the classroom to juggle the urge to check in with each of the children while committing to one child's or one group's play experience, it is important that the teachers allow themselves to step into a child's world and join in as a full participant in play in order to scaffold learning.

- Large-group time is an exciting part of our daily routine during which the children enjoy a wide range of engaging activities. I have found that it's equally important to include the tried-and-true favorites as well as some new activities. Along these lines, I've found it also works well to include variations of familiar large-group movement and music experiences, to keep children and teachers excited about sharing large-group experiences together.

- Planning can be supported throughout various parts of the daily routine — not just during planning time. Teachers who choose strategies that work well for their small groups can also encourage meaningful planning by scaffolding during recall, as well as during work time when children begin to transition into new plans. Further, whenever children grow excited about certain materials, teachers can make a note to use these materials during planning time and/or to remind the children that they may make a plan to use the materials during work time that day or the following day.

Chapter 9

Fine-Tuning

March

1

Thursday

Parent Meeting About Power Struggles

What went well?

This week we had our second meeting for parents. We try to host a family-oriented event every month (e.g., a field trip, home visit, or parent-teacher conference). As part of that, we may try to have a group parent meeting every other month or so. At our first parent meeting, we had focused on active learning — something that is especially important for parents who are new to HighScope — and this time we talked about power struggles. This was very timely, as we have seen a rise in such struggles between children and adults lately, whether during our own daily routine or between children and their parents before and after school. This was also a topic selected by parents when we queried them about discussion topics at the beginning of the school year.

Parents share their thoughts about their child's development in a meeting with teachers at the Demonstration Preschool.

Building on what I already know

By merely helping to present the issue of power struggles at the parent meeting, I gained a better understanding of this issue. Here are the basics of what we covered on the topic of power struggles, and how we connected classroom ideas to home life:

- **Setting limits and offering choices with children at home:** At school, we acknowledge feelings and talk about the problem. We also work together with children to come up with possible solutions. At home when a problem arises, family members can describe the child's action or feelings, explain the reason for setting a limit, and offer choices relating to a possible solution. For example, if a child doesn't want to wear a hat in the winter, an adult can say, "I know that you don't want to wear a hat (acknowledging), but we need to wear something to keep our head warm and safe in the winter (describing and giving a reason for the limit-setting). You can choose to wear your blue hat or your hood (giving choices)."

- **Sharing control and giving choices:** As in the classroom, giving children simple, manageable choices at home helps children feel a sense of control. We also want to empower children to make decisions. There are times when adults can offer open-ended choices, and other times when choices are more limited.

- **Communicating:** When adults say what they mean in a positive way (stating what children *can* do rather than what they *can't* do), it is easier for children to understand what needs to be done. For example, instead of saying "Don't run in the classroom/in the house," adults can say, "You can walk in the house and run outside." It's also important for adults to express feelings to children using "I" statements such as "I feel frustrated because you are walking away while we are trying to solve the problem." This lets children know how adults feel about the problem while also modeling language that shows ownership of (responsibility for) feelings. Children may also need a space in which to calm down their bodies and emotions; this is an option at school as well as at home.

- **Natural consequences:** In the classroom, if the children have difficulty with cleanup time, they understand that we might not have enough time to read a story at snacktime. They know that if they don't wear mittens outside, their hands will get cold. Teaching children about consequences like these can also take place at home, and families can use these as active learning opportunities for children in which choice is involved.

In cases in which children are acting out strong emotions, remember to acknowledge feelings and discuss the problem, using the six steps to conflict resolution.

The Screen-Time Debate

Ideas and insights

We have had a couple of parents and visitors to the classroom ask us about the appropriateness of using computers in our preschool program and how much screen time is okay for young children. I struggle with this question myself. On one hand, I want children to become engaged with the more traditional materials in our classroom. I want children to have ample opportunities to look at books, to role play in pretend scenarios, and to manipulate objects and materials as they explore and create. However, I also want the children to have experiences with tools and technology while problem solving and collaborating.

Some children love the computers. I help this child be intentional in his computer use by talking to him about how he is implementing his work-time plan.

Technology in our classroom. The way we use technology in our classroom may be different from the way it is handled in other programs. I do want to stress that my use of the phrase "screen time" here refers only to computers. Some programs use tablets and other devices, but we do not have those. We also don't show children movies or television programs. Of course, the category "tools and technology" includes many devices that are not the media items that immediately come to mind; however, the specific topic of concern here is about the use of computers in our preschool.

Decisions about technology use. There are some important things to consider when making decisions about the use of technology. We do want to consider the children's interests. We have children who choose to use the computers and are generally interested in them as a material in the classroom. We also want to respect that some parents of children in our classroom want to limit their child's screen time. It often happens that these are the parents of the children most drawn to the computers. Obviously, it's very important to consider the children's needs on an individual basis. Last year we had a few children who probably were not exposed to computers at home, and we certainly did not want to eliminate their opportunity to explore this technology. This year, I am pretty sure that all the children's families have computers at home, but we do still have the computers available as a choice in the book area.

Building on what I already know

Technology and active learning. While reflecting on our students' needs regarding technology use, it's important for me to consider HighScope's approach; particularly the components of active learning. The five ingredients of active learning are materials; manipulation; choice; child communication, language, and thought; and adult scaffolding.

- **Materials:** This year, we have been offering computers as a classroom material since January. In other words, we chose not to bring out the computers until the children had had experiences with more traditional materials (e.g., blocks, dolls, play dough, puzzles, paint, cooking items, books). We also don't want the computers to take away from children's other work-time experiences. We have two computers, each with a different developmentally appropriate game loaded on it. We rotate out the games periodically, and bring in new ones, but we haven't been changing the games very often lately because we wanted to try out a new strategy: seeing what would happen if we didn't draw extra attention to the computers.

- **Manipulation:** We offer children computer games that are open ended and allow the user to move about among various parts of the game. For example, if it's a virtual book, they can move backward from page to page and click on the interactive features. Or they may stay on a screen and "paint" something or write using the keyboard.

- **Choice:** The children have a choice about whether they want to use the computers and how to use them. Sometimes they pretend that they are businessmen and businesswomen working in the book area, and they need computers to do their "homework" or other work. Sometimes the children will ask to use specific games on the computers. Children can also choose how to manipulate this material as suggested above under "Manipulation."

- **Child communication, language, and thought:** It's amazing how much of a collaborative experience using the computers can be. We place several chairs around the monitors in hopes of facilitating collaboration. When the children use the computers, they talk together about what's happening and explain to one another and the teachers how the games work. They solve problems together. They also use the computers to convey messages, describe things, and read together; and they also sign up for turns on the computers.

- **Adult scaffolding:** When adults are present to support and acknowledge the children's choices, as well as to talk with the children involved, the use of the computer becomes a more meaningful experience.

What support do I need?

I'm still not completely comfortable with computers in the preschool classroom. But I think that, as with anything else, it's all about balance. Computers are not a mandatory part of our HighScope Demonstration Preschool program; rather, it is a choice we offer children in limited amounts. As I have mentioned, Clyde is a child who has spent more time on the computers than some other children. Together with his family, we have decided to support him by asking him to make more than one choice at planning time, by encouraging him to move on to his second plan after first using a computer during work time, and by helping him replan as needed. When we give him the support he needs, he is able to self-monitor his screen time for the most part.

Interestingly, the National Association for the Education of Young Children (NAEYC) recently adopted a position statement on the use of technology in early childhood programs: "Technology and interactive media are tools that can promote effective learning and development when they are used intentionally by early childhood educators within the framework of developmentally appropriate practices to support learning goals established for individual children" (NAEYC, 2012, p. 5).* The words in this statement that stand out to me are *intentionally* and *developmentally appropriate*. If we are choosing to introduce the computers and open-ended software programs in ways that allow for active learning, including scaffolding and interaction, the use of computers *can* be an asset to the children's educational experiences.

It feels supportive when Shannon and I talk about these issues when "debriefing" at the end of the day, during our planning sessions. Also, I spend a lot of time talking to some concerned parents about technology in the classroom — especially Clyde and Fatima's mothers, both of whom are concerned about screen time. We have come up with ideas together, such as helping the children to be more intentional in their planning.

March

16
Friday

Very Active Learning

What did I notice about the children?

Children enjoy moving their bodies and exploring gross-motor movements and activities. Our children have the opportunity to move their bodies throughout the day — most obviously during large-group time and outside time. However, we also encourage gross-motor movement during transitions and work time, and sometimes during small-group time, planning time, and recall time as well.

---

*National Association for the Education of Young Children. (8 May, 2012). [Position paper]. "Technology and Media as Interactive Tools in Early Childhood Programs Serving Children from Birth Through Age 8." Retrieved from http://issuu.com/naeyc/docs/ps_technology_issuu_may2012?mode=window&backgroundColor=%23222222

Some children choose to move their bodies during work time, and we strive to have appropriate materials available in the classroom to support these choices safely. For example, we have large blocks to build and climb on, soft balls to throw, and miniature toy cars or mini toy skateboards with ramps that children can use to explore movement. We also have Sit 'n Spins, rotators, and

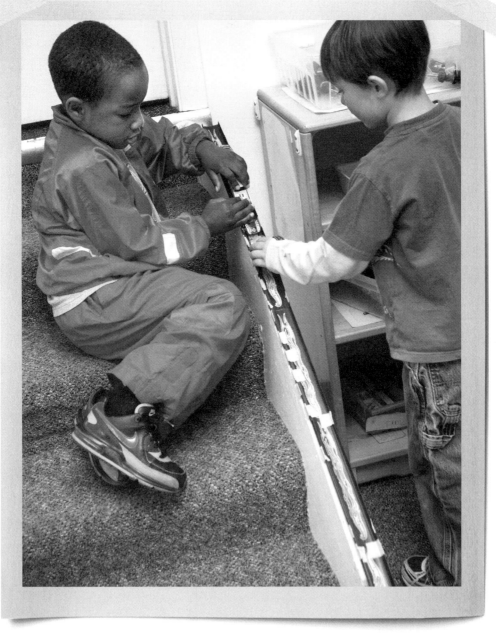

Using miniature toy cars on an incline is one way that children can safely explore movement in the classroom.

cushions. In addition, we have items that children use as props when taking on roles in pretend play — for example, books, leashes, uniforms, flashlights, and steering wheels, which the children use for pretending to be dogs, car drivers, spies, and more.

Ideas and insights

Adult participation. Since I have been teaching at the Demonstration Pre-school, there have been times when I've questioned what I might *allow* the children to do during various parts of the daily routine. I have explored the delicate balance between supporting the children's choices (while talking through possible problems or my concerns) and letting the children do what-ever they want. Of course the latter is not my intention, but I think about that range of strategies as I strive to consider what is best.

I have found that it's important for me to consider safety, of course, but also to ask myself why I might think something is unsafe. Sometimes I have realized that an initial twinge of concern about a child's choice is only a link back to my previous understandings about the rules often employed in ele-mentary settings, or a notion about "the way it has always been done." When-ever I realize that that's the case, I take it upon myself to consider whether my involvement, including scaffolding the children's activity, will eliminate the fear there. For example, there are some teachers who express fears that when children stack the large, hollow blocks as high as the children can reach, the blocks, which are heavy, could fall on the children. However, if an adult is present, he or she can collaborate with the children to maintain a safe building experience. The same could be said of children's use of the materials in our woodworking area. The children safely use tools with safety glasses and adult support after being introduced to the materials during a small-group time.

Expressing concerns. If the children choose to do something I'm con-cerned about, after I do some self-reflection, my next step is to express my concern to the children so we can talk about it together and come up with so-lutions to any problems. For example, I might say, "Fatima, you want to climb on the blocks. I'm worried that this stack of blocks is not sturdy enough and it's not safe for your body." The children respond to my explanations of my feel-ings of anxiety, and we are able to work through the problem together. I listen to the children's ideas, and then I sometimes add ideas of my own, such as, "I wonder if we could add more blocks so it's safer." We use this same problem-solving process when children want to throw materials. We have materials available (soft crocheted balls, foam balls, scarves, etc.) that children can use to throw so they can experience that movement. Nevertheless, there are certainly times when we must remind the children that it's just not a safe choice to throw certain things. Another example is running in the classroom — there's not enough space to move safely indoors, so running is an outside choice.

Following children's lead. Today Declan decided that he wanted to play football. He approached me after planning, during work time, and he was very excited to show me the jersey that he had put on. "You need one too," he said. "You wanna play with me?" Declan and I found a few more child-sized jerseys, and I put on the largest one I could find. He directed me over to the book area (where we have a bit of open space near the stairs that lead up to our conference room), and we began to talk about what we would do. "So what do we do first?" I asked. "Okay," said Declan, "You got to throw the ball and I'll catch it." He pointed toward where I should stand, and he went up on the third of four gentle steps to wait for my pass. I tossed the ball to Declan. He caught the ball, then climbed down the steps and moved a few steps past me to the couch where he shouted "Touchdown!" I realized I never thought I'd be playing football in the classroom but asked myself, Why not? Declan was able to explore an interest in a game with rules and engage in large-motor movement (KDI 16. Gross-motor skills, and KDI 18. Body awareness, in curriculum content area C. Physical Development and Health). Soon enough, Kyra and Clyde joined in our play, and Declan helped to successfully maintain their involvement for the remainder of work time.

We made Declan's play safe for him by choosing a larger area, yet not so large that there was room for him to run. I did have to remind him to be careful of the children who were nearby using the computers, but I wasn't too concerned because Declan was using a small, soft ball. When Kyra and Clyde joined in, Declan explained to them how the game was played and added that everyone needed to be careful about moving from the steps to the couch. We took turns throwing and catching. Additionally, when I was trying to "tag" Declan on defense, I did not rush after him. When Declan was trying to tag me, I moved slowly then too. Thus, in this way, the tone of the game was set by my movements.

What I Learned This Month

Here are some conclusions I've drawn from my own active learning experiences this month:

- Parent meetings are one way to get to know families and teach them about the HighScope Curriculum, as well as to create opportunities for families to share concerns and ideas with one another. Family members are often particularly interested in information on shared control, setting limits, and offering choices. Sharing more about why and how HighScope uses these strategies in the classroom, and recognizing and facilitating a discussion about how families might adopt and adapt such strategies, solidifies a team effort between parents and teachers.

- As with anything else, maintaining a balance when offering children screen time can benefit both school and home environments. If materials such as computers or iPads are available in the classroom, teachers can consider and plan how their groups of children might use and benefit from such materials (just as with any other classroom material). Open-ended games or applications keep the focus on active learning central to the curriculum.

- Young children enjoy active experiences that engage them in gross-motor movement activities. The urge to run around, throw materials, jump, and dance about the classroom are normal and exciting ideas for preschoolers. Teachers who keep an open mind about how to safely allow for such experiences throughout the day, while incorporating safe materials with which to engage in such activities (as well as setting necessary limits), can honor children's ideas and elicit new ones about how to adapt an activity for the indoor classroom.

Chapter 10

Making Connections

Materials in the Classroom

Ideas and insights

Teaching at the Demonstration Preschool has opened my eyes to the endless options for materials that can be used in the preschool classroom. Most of my prior teaching experience had been with early elementary students, but I had also been fortunate to have had a wonderful teaching experience in a high-quality, early childhood program (that was accredited by the National Association for the Education of Young Children [NAEYC]) a couple of years before coming to HighScope. In that program as at HighScope, children are offered a plentiful supply of a wide range of materials, which are organized by area.

At the HighScope Demonstration Preschool, we have a basic set of materials that we keep in the classroom throughout the course of the year. In the house area, we have pots, pans, cups, plates, bowls, measuring cups, cookbooks, silverware, baby dolls and related items, some dress-up clothes, shoes, and wardrobe accessories. In the art area, we have paint and brushes, paper, markers, glue, scissors, tape, and play dough. The book area always has books, puzzles, and writing materials and cozy spaces for using these materials. Because our block area is spacious, right now it is not only full of small solid-wood blocks and large, hollow blocks, but it also includes a variety of musical instruments that children often use to make a band. In this area we also keep a few different kinds of soft balls that children can throw indoors without harm. The sand and water table is always available to children and includes scoops and toys with which children can explore the sand and water. We keep magnetic tiles, people figures, shells, trains, and Legos or Duplos in the toy area.

We also rotate in materials that complement our base set of materials and add to children's open-ended play. For example, we put strainers and cupcake pans in the house area, sponges to use with paint and cookie cutters in the art area, games and 3-D puzzles in the book area, cars and a dollhouse in the block area, animals and dinosaurs in the toy area, and different types of measuring cups at the sand and water table. We also add the woodworking area to the classroom mid-year.

Found, recycled, and household materials

In addition to these materials, we have added some that I had never before thought of using. A visit to the Scrapbox, a local recycled materials store, helps us give the children even more choices — we rotate in bins of reused bottle caps, cardboard rolls, plastic pieces, corks, and empty containers. Of course, similar items can be collected at home as well. Other examples of found, recycled, or real/household materials include old cell phones, clothes, keyboards, steering wheels, flashlights, keys, household kitchen items, baby clothes, and paper towel tubes. I have found myself collecting things from around the house and picking up more materials at the local secondhand shops.

Natural and homemade materials

Natural and homemade materials are also important to add to the learning environment. We usually keep shells, pine cones, and rocks in the classroom. I've started collecting things around our playground and in my own yard. This year, we have added leaves, sticks, wood, seed pods, and pistachio shells (we don't have any children with nut allergies this year) to the art area. When a tree was cut from our playground, we added cut slices of branches to the block area (for stacking and building) and to the art area (for gluing and making sculptures). Beans, rice, dirt, and other sensory items have spent time in our sand and water table as well. We've also made a push to work with more loose materials and natural materials outside — for example, large tubes, boxes, Styrofoam pieces, wreaths, seeds and plants for a garden, and much more. A few homemade materials that we have used have included photo albums, musical shakers made with beans or rice, melted chunky crayons, "community blocks" (sturdy boxes with photographs of local buildings taped onto them), and "popcorn" balls made of sponges.

The children and I hop between moveable "tree cookies." These were made from a felled tree trunk that was cut into slices.

Using materials throughout the routine

What's interesting is how we have been able to weave these materials and their open-ended uses into small-group time or planning and recall times. A particular favorite of mine is reusing cookie tins or coffee cans for the "Story in a Can" activity (developed by HighScope Field Consultant and former Demonstration Preschool teacher Julie Austin). Putting some materials in the can (such as people figures, Cuisenaire rods, rocks, a piece of fabric, tiles, and a other small toys) and then telling a story with the pieces inside is a fun way to explore pretending, language, and collaborative play with the children, who often build stories off of one another.

Materials and content areas

Here are some reflections on how open-ended materials can foster children's learning in the different content areas:

A. Approaches to Learning

Using a wide variety of interesting materials (many different types of materials that cater to children's various interests and developmental levels) fosters engagement. Children will show initiative with materials that they are eager to explore.

B. Social and Emotional Development

As children discover and explore with materials, their excitement and confidence grows. They may also engage in play with other children and adults, working together to build, create, or otherwise experiment with the materials provided.

C. Physical Development and Health

Open-ended indoor and outdoor materials that foster physical development are often used in other content areas as well. Materials ranging from items as big as tricycles and climbers to smaller items like balls and scarves may be used throughout the routine: plan-do-review, small-group time, large-group time, and outside times.

D. Language, Literacy, and Communication

Most any material imaginable can relate to this content area. This is because active learning incorporates not only child language and thought, but also language development through adult scaffolding. Specific examples of materials that foster learning in this area include books, letters (wooden, magnetic, or stickers), paper and writing tools, and puppets. In addition to sparking conversations that include shared vocabulary, these materials often lead to reading, writing, singing, and storytelling, as well as a variety of nonverbal communications.

E. Mathematics

Like language, math is involved in so much of children's play. When children explore, they work with concepts such as angle, size, similarity and difference, counting, sorting, spatial awareness, and measuring. Materials for exploring math concepts include the following:

- *Number words and symbols:* message board, magnetic numerals, number stamps and stickers

- *Counting:* counting bears, shells, figures, blocks

- *Part-whole relationships:* blocks and magnetic tiles

- *Shape:* shape blocks, foam blocks, puzzles, paper and scissors, floor shapes, tracings

- *Spatial reasoning:* puzzles, stacking blocks, climbers, train tracks with train set

- *Measuring:* tape measures, measuring cups, scoops, recycled containers, kitchen items

- *Unit:* measuring materials, Unifix cubes, yarn

- *Pattern:* any materials children can place in a row and make patterns with, such as Unifix cubes and Cuisenaire rods

- *Data analysis:* books, photos, message board, recipes, daily routine cards; graphs made at or for planning, recall, or small-group time

F. Creative Arts

The children use all of the classroom materials in their pretend play! They incorporate materials in both expected and unexpected ways. For example, a child might use small stones, corks, or shells in building with blocks, storytelling, scooping pretend cement with diggers at the sand table or outside, gluing in the art area, or cooking in the house area. In addition, children use a multitude of materials to explore art and music in numerous ways. They also use these in conjunction with other content areas, for example, when children use a parachute (gross-motor physical development skill) and move it to music while keeping a beat (math and music).

G. Science and Technology

Children observe, classify, and experiment with all kinds of materials. As they do this, they test their previous notions and confirm new and/or previous ideas. Specific examples of materials that foster learning in this area include different sizes and types of blocks; paint, clay, and play dough; musical instruments; materials for moving with music, such as scarves or ribbons; balls; sand-and-water-table materials; and plants and other natural items.

H. Social Studies

When children explore materials outside and inside the classroom, they do so in the context of their understanding of roles in the classroom and community. They play out such roles and make classroom decisions together about how to use materials in their play, whether building, pretending, or otherwise exploring. Materials that foster learning in this area include diverse dolls — of different races, genders, and ages, and representing different community roles (for example, dolls clothed in a doctor jacket, firefighter hat, or construction helmet).

April

16

Monday

Using the COR to Support Children

Ideas and insights

As I've mentioned, I had worked in a number of classrooms before coming to the HighScope Demonstration Preschool. Unfortunately, in some of these programs — mainly at the early elementary level — children were subjected to rigorous and developmentally inappropriate testing. This is why I feel so strongly about the Child Observation Record (COR), which we use to assess the developmental progress of our preschoolers. My teaching partner, Shannon, and I take daily notes, also referred to as anecdotal records, on the chil-

I write an anecdote as I observe and engage with children in the book area.

dren in our program. We jot down real-life, objective anecdotes about what we see and hear the children doing and saying throughout the year. At the end of each day, we enter these anecdotes into the OnlineCOR program. This program collects our anecdotes and organizes them by date and COR items.

Building on what I already know

A manual COR kit is also available, but the online program saves time and adds many features such as cross-referencing of students and COR items, and it includes assessment graphs to monitor how well the children are progressing (both individually and by class) and how well we are tracking their development.

Even after starting work at HighScope, I didn't become familiar with the extra features of the OnlineCOR until I enrolled in the HighScope online course "Using COR Data to Inform Instruction." As I progressed through the course, I was able to play around with the various components of the online program. Not only are there sections for parent involvement and lesson planning, but there are a number of reports that can be generated to view how the class is progressing and how the children are progressing individually.

Using these reports helps us see a picture of the overall data as well as a variety of more in-depth views. Before I participated in the Using COR Data course, I had been using anecdotes to observe the children and keep a record of their development. Toward the end of each evaluation period, and some time before parent-teacher conferences, Shannon and I sit down and evaluate the children's development. We also think about which areas we need to support and assess more often as we prepare our daily plans. Now that I have had the experience of creating reports that show gains, monitor growth, and help us track how well we are observing our children, I am better equipped to use this information to inform my practice. (For an overview of the KDIs and COR, see p. 12.)

Shannon takes anecdotal notes on what she observes children in her small group doing.

What I Learned This Month

Here are some conclusions I've drawn from my own active learning experiences this month:

- Materials in the preschool classroom can range from purchased traditional wooden blocks to seashells collected at the beach to sandpaper to pots and pans to much, much, more! I will never look at an everyday material the same way again. I enjoyed finding creative ways to bring found, recycled, natural, and everyday materials into the various areas of the classroom for use throughout the daily routine. What's more, sometimes when I was unsure of how the children would use the materials, or whether they would use them at all, I found their creativity with them to be truly ingenious!

- Using an assessment tool like the COR is a wonderful way to observe and record the children's progress. Further, it not only helps me record meaningful anecdotes about the children's development but also to plan ahead for scaffolding children's learning.

Chapter 11

Problem Solving at the End of the Year

May
3
Thursday

Experiences With Visitor-Observers

Ideas and insights

About twice a month, visitors observe our classroom at the Demonstration Preschool via live-feed video from the adjoining conference room. It's a special opportunity for viewers to see the HighScope Curriculum in action without disrupting the children's day. After children have left for the day, Shannon and I create a plan for the following school day as observers take the opportunity to ask us questions and discuss situations that relate to their own experiences. We also give them a classroom tour so they can get a good look at the materials, areas, and setup of the learning environment.

Visitors are often interested in talking about anecdote-writing. Anecdotes are short vignettes we write down that illustrate children's development, and which we later enter into our Child Observation Record (COR) files (for more on anecdotes, see p. 20; for more on the COR, see pp. 164–167). Visitors are also very interested in the materials in our classroom, which I've discussed at greater length in my April 10 entry (pp. 159–164). Other big talking points with classroom visitors include the real kitchen items and food containers that we have in the house area, the homemade and natural materials placed through-out the room, and the structure of the sand and water table, with its tubes, compartments, and pulleys.

Every day this week we have had visitors who are here for the High-Scope International Conference (held each May here in Ypsilanti, not far from HighScope's headquarters). These observers were interested in our activity bags — a strategy for home-school connections that I gave a presentation on at the conference this week. (For more on activity bags, see p. 133.) These kits include a book and some open-ended materials that help children and parents explore active learning at home.

Building on what I already know

This week, some of the conference attendees visiting our classroom began talking to me about problem solving with children. I had an in-depth conversa-tion with some of them following preschool this morning. They were wonder-ing if I could talk more about a particular conflict that occurred today between Miriam and Mina. During work time today, Mina was pretending to be a prin-cess in a castle and had grown rather upset because she wanted Miriam to join her. Miriam had been interested in playing with Mina, but didn't want to be a pretend princess. Mina, strong in her own right, hadn't wanted to wander off with Miriam and do something else. I had acknowledged both girls' feelings and had tried to learn more about what they each wanted to do. I'd ended up saying something like "It sounds like the two of you have different plans — and that's okay." The visitor was interested in hearing more about how I had decided to phrase my response.

I think it's hard for us as adults to stretch our thinking about situations like this. Sometimes, because we want children to be happy and get along with one another, we almost want to tell them to "just play together and be friends." However, in this situation, it was certainly appropriate for Miriam to choose what she wanted to do. We may feel that we would like her to join and comfort Mina, but Miriam should certainly be able to pursue her own interests and be supported in doing so.

Children collaborate at the sand and water table while maintaining their pretend-play roles.

May

8

Tuesday

Work Time Through a New Lens

Ideas and insights

This year, HighScope's early childhood department acquired a few digital cameras with which trainers could record videos of various parts of the classroom routine while training in other settings. It wasn't until recently that someone recommended we try using one in the Demonstration Preschool classroom. It was an interesting suggestion, and one that I decided to follow up on today. I was especially eager to do this since, whenever we have visitors observing at the Demonstration Preschool, I always hear about something interesting that I missed during work time because I was across the room engaged with children in a completely different scenario. I had tried using the camera once to get the whole picture of how a small-group time went, but this time I wanted to see what I was missing while I was away from the camera. So I set up the camera on a table and let it record the scene.

What did I observe about the children?

Mason and the paints. In one segment of the footage I shot, Mason talks to me about his painting in the art area, and I talk to him about how he got green paint. "You *know*, Becky!" he says to me, and we laugh, because by now he knows that I understand how to mix primary colors.

Kyra, Nikki, Fatima, and the tree-cutouts. Meanwhile, in the background of this same segment, Kyra explains to Nikki how to cut out a tree. She holds a pair of scissors in one hand and wrapping paper with trees printed on it in the other. "First you cut to get up to the star, and then you go down and down and down and down and then you cut off here," Kyra explains. Then she reaches her hands up in the air and proudly displays her tree: "Ta-dah! How you cut out a Christmas tree!" she exclaims. Afterward, one can spot Fatima getting some wrapping paper and scissors. She comes back to the table and starts singing "I'm going to cut a Christmas tree, a Christmas tree…" It is interesting to see how Fatima took the lead from Kyra when the two were not interacting directly, and I find this even more interesting since the girls have been having quite a few conflicts with one another. This was a rare opportunity to watch them working side by side — Kyra so intently choosing her materials and teaching anyone who will listen, and Fatima imitating those choices.

Fatima's extension. Later in the video footage, I see Fatima extending the paper-tree-cutting play by getting out her own, different materials and using scissors to cut tape several times. As I watch, seeing that she can work the tape dispenser so easily surprises me. She pulls and cuts the tape four different times, even successfully pulling up the tape when it gets stuck on the dispenser after the second cut. The last time I observed Fatima with the tape, which must have been a couple of weeks prior, she had expressed frustration as the tape had twisted around itself.

Food mix for Lavender Bunny. After a while, the scene blurs as we move the camera to the other side of the room, where Miriam, Clyde, and Avery are at the sand and water table having a conversation about Lavender Bunny, a stuffed animal that Miriam has at home. She often interweaves stories about her bunny into her conversations and her play. The children are digging in the sand and talking about vegetables Lavender Bunny might want to eat. "Nope, not lettuce," says Miriam, "Lavender Bunny hates it." Clyde replies, "Well, maybe carrots...." "Nope, not even carrots," Miriam retorts.

Then Clyde starts talking about grubs, which I find interesting because he brought them up during snacktime too. Soon the children start mixing some food for the bunny. Miriam says to Clyde and Avery, "Bring me everything, and I'll start mixing. Bring me everything except for the carrots." Avery chimes in, "I have a whole bucket of different things." At this point, Liam pops over and starts watching from a few feet away. He just quietly stands there, and I wonder if he's hoping to join in since he's been playing with Avery quite a bit lately.

All the while, the boys are scooping and dumping and taking some measuring cups to Miriam, who has the shovel and the container on the floor where they're doing the mixing. Avery asks Clyde, "Hey, can I have my spot back?" while sort of pushing him aside with his hip. Clyde nudges back but sort of giggles about it and says in a silly voice, "Hey can I have *my* spot back?" Then he says, "I have grubs coming down and I have rotten carrots!" taking them to Miriam's mix. It was pleasant to watch the children playfully and creatively interacting, and to see Clyde step around a potential problem by using his sense of humor.

May

14

Monday

Problem-Solving Opportunities

Ideas and insights

The end of the school year is approaching, and we certainly do not lack for problem-solving opportunities. I like thinking of them in just that way: as *opportunities*. Certainly, these situations can arise during moments when we, as teachers, feel on edge. There are also times when such moments can leave us pleasantly dumbfounded and amazed with the children's creativity. Other days, such conflicts can leave us exhausted and practicing taking deep breaths.

What did I observe about the children?

Today was "one of those days" — the children seemed to have one problem after another. It started during planning time when I was still planning with Fatima. Declan had already begun using the large, hollow blocks in the block area, and Veronica came to me upset, saying "Declan won't let me use any of the blocks!" As soon as Fatima heard this, she became angry because that meant she wouldn't have any blocks either. When I walked the girls over to the block area to help solve the problem, Clyde and Avery joined in the argument as well — they needed blocks for playing "Star Wars" with Mina and Nikki. Hearing these arguments, Declan stormed off to the book area at the far end of the room. He made a pouting face and crossed his arms over his chest.

Declan has knowledge and experience in problem solving, but lately he hasn't been drawing on his skills in this area. I wanted to take some time to reflect and try to discover what may be at the root of this. After school today I spoke with Declan's mom. She has been worried about his behaviors as well. We worked through some questions together: Is Declan immediately on the defense because he has grown accustomed to being the one "in trouble"? Is he losing patience since he knows how long it can take for children (especially those in earlier stages of development) to solve problems? Has Declan "checked out" because he is more ready for kindergarten? The process of writing this first and then talking with Declan's mom has really helped me to work through my thoughts on this matter.

I work with some children involved in a conflict over how many blocks each child will use.

Follow-Up to "Problem-Solving Opportunities"

What did I observe about the children?

Today we brought the cardboard blocks from our storage space in the basement, to add another building material to the block area. It was our hope that adding this material might give children ideas about alternative choices to the very popular large, hollow blocks, and it did help for the children to have an even wider range of materials to choose from. In addition, I really made an effort to acknowledge Declan when he needed to be heard today. Work time began with Fatima yelling at him for knocking over blocks, so I took the

Important Notes

Journal Writing and Talking to Parents

I generally find that it's very helpful to write down my observations, thoughts, insights, and ideas as soon as possible. In fact, I have found it really helpful to write out my thoughts both before and after talking to a parent — as I recently did when talking to Declan's mom. Putting ideas down in my own words helped me to really reflect on what we've tried, what's worked well, and what has been a challenge for Declan in our classroom. What's more, working through my ideas about Declan's situation helped me to organize my thoughts so that I had a better idea of how to facilitate a meaningful conversation with Declan's mother. That is, because I had first spent time reflecting on this so deeply, I was able to respond to Declan's mom not only with well-prepared answers but also with greater overall insight. When she shared her thoughts, I was better able to receive her ideas, process them in the moment, and react thoughtfully. Thus, we were able to work through the problem as a parent-teacher team.

opportunity to talk Declan through it. I wanted him to know that, even though I wanted to talk to him about this problem involving Fatima, he was not "in trouble." I explained this to him and continued to acknowledge his feelings of frustration.

I also confronted Fatima while making sure that Declan could observe this. I wanted to acknowledge Fatima's frustrations and sadness about her blocks falling down, but I also wanted to let her know that it's not okay to yell at Declan and to help her see that it made Declan sad when she blamed him. We were able to resolve the issue, and she and Declan continued to work in the same area.

What I Learned This Month

Here are some conclusions I've drawn from my own active learning experiences this month:

- Having observers in our classroom brings about many opportunities to discuss curriculum highlights with those who have questions about the HighScope Curriculum. Answering curriculum questions from observers, volunteers, families, or other educators can be challenging for teachers. However, talking through situations with interested adults from various backgrounds can help teachers to understand more about the curriculum and even their own philosophies.

- Video recording my teaching proved to be a valuable tool for self-observation and reflection. However teachers choose to reflect on their days or weeks, it is important to set aside time to do this regularly. The practice of wondering, thinking, asking questions, and challenging myself has helped me to grow in so many ways. Lifelong learning is important for children and adults alike!

- Problem-solving opportunities undoubtedly arise each and every day in the preschool classroom, but with the right tools in the six steps, we can support children in positive problem-solving experiences. What's more, as children grow in this process, they will become skilled problem solvers with creative and clever solutions to issues that arise. They will carry these skills with them throughout their lives.

Chapter 12

Rich Interactions at the End of the School Year

June

1

Friday

Work Time Outside

What went well?

The weather has been so warm and lovely these past couple of weeks, and today we decided to take work time outside. When Shannon and I first started talking about the idea, I sort of thought of it as an extended outside time. We have a great number of materials in our shed outdoors and a growing number of "loose parts" (e.g., sections of plastic drainage gutters, large cardboard tubes, tires) as well. Shannon helped to shape the idea with her suggestion that we roll out the art cart. This got us thinking about how we could try to have materials from each area outdoors, even though we wouldn't have exactly set areas.

  Taking materials outdoors. We started with the new art easels, and the tempera cakes of paint with water were perfect for transporting outside. We rolled out the art cart, which houses our markers, scissors, play dough, paper, tape, and the like. On the blacktop, we set out some toy area materials —

Duplos, magnetic tiles, and horses. Sue, my mentor, came by in the morning and said she thought the carpet squares would be a nice addition, so that the children would feel comfortable sitting and working in the outdoor space.

Before the day began, we took the large, wooden stacking planks (they are sort of like giant Lincoln Logs) out of the shed and brought out a bin of the cardboard blocks. We set cars out by the handicapped access ramp (which is not in use except when visitors come or when families are arriving or leaving at the beginning or end of the day), and prepared the outdoor water table and its materials. We took puzzles out to one of the picnic tables, we rolled the wagon of sand toys (pots, pans, buckets, scoops, shovels, and the like) out to the sandbox, and we added a blanket to a shaded area under two nearby trees with a bin of books. Finally, we set the hammers, nails, and safety glasses next to a trio of tree stumps. I started to get pretty excited about our day!

Building on what I already know

Being outside took the children's work time to a new level. They were excited to be in a "new" work time environment, even though we had kept changes to a minimum by only bringing out materials that the children use regularly indoors. Here is some of the complex play we observed.

Cars and ramps. Declan took the cars up the handicapped access ramp outside the preschool building and spent the entire time racing the cars down the ramp. Avery and Liam joined him, and the boys were shouting with excitement about how fast the cars were moving, how far down they could go, and whether they flipped over or not. It was neat to watch them using the cars in such an open space.

Tools and tree bark. Mason started using the hammers and nails on the fallen tree trunk. When he hammered a nail on the loose bark, he squatted down and examined it, noticing that he could still see the nail because the bark was loose. He started pulling the bark up a bit and I helped him pull it back further. Fatima came over to join us.

Liam was also watching, and he approached as Mason and Fatima continued to pull back more of the bark. The children were excited about this new discovery. They were finding "roly-poly" insects underneath the bark, and they found some ants too. They turned the hammers and twisted their tools to get a better grip on the bark as they worked at pulling it up. The children were so intrigued!

As I support children and scaffold their learning, the children inspect, hammer, and pull up loose bark from a downed tree trunk in the playground during an outdoor work time.

Next Kyra and Avery joined in, wondering what the other children were doing. They started working on the bark of the tree stump beside the log. Hundreds of ants started crawling out as they pulled back the bark, and more children came over to check it out. There was some problem solving involved when I began to wonder if the ants would bite the children and Veronica started to cry because some of the children wanted to smash the ants with hammers. Another child agreed we should take care of the ants, and so we all slowed to observe them. As the children's engagement shifted from action to observation and discussion, Veronica's and my worries were alleviated. We stopped to take a closer look at the inside of the bark, and the children discovered the insect pathways that were visible on both the bark and the bare tree trunk.

What I Learned This Month

Here are some conclusions I've drawn from my own active learning experiences this month:

- Taking work time outside is a delightful way for the children to experience this part of the day, as well as both indoor and outdoor materials, in a new way. Work time outdoors can be especially successful since the children love being outside (especially for an extended period of time). Bringing to the outdoor area typical indoor materials — such as hammers from the woodworking area — brings new opportunities and excitement to work time for the children.

Children observe and talk about what they've discovered underneath the bark.

A structure the children made when work time materials were taken outdoors.

Chapter 13

Reflections

A New Perspective on HighScope Fundamentals

Since I began using the HighScope Curriculum over a year ago, my thoughts on the various elements of the curriculum have grown as my professional development and experiences have progressed. As I move forward, I continue to question and reflect. Some ideas shift, change, and further develop. Others, however, are now a permanent part of my philosophy and mission to remain an educator and advocate for developmentally appropriate early childhood practices. What follows are my reflections on the HighScope Curriculum after my first full year of teaching at the Demonstration Preschool. The categories below correspond to the topics I wrote about in Chapter 1, a follow-up to my first six weeks of teaching for HighScope.

Shared control

Early on, I remember struggling to grasp what this really meant — sharing control with the children. I had a hard time understanding how to appropriately give children control without giving them too much control. Over time, I've learned how to integrate more *choice* — one of the key ingredients of active learning — into each classroom experience. Giving children a voice in what they will explore, how they will play and learn, who they will collaborate with, what *their* classroom should look like, how to express themselves, and, essentially, how to create their own preschool experience makes their world come together for them. It makes their learning meaningful. Giving children a sense of control in the classroom helps them understand what a vital role they play in their personal community. I have always understood that young learners are capable; knowing this, one of my main goals has always been to promote responsibility. Shared control in the classroom takes such expectations even further. Supporting children as they make child-sized decisions helps them grow as responsible citizens who will become capable of expressing themselves, thinking critically, solving problems, empathizing with others, and making sure they are heard. Balancing these choices with appropriate teacher decisions (such as what materials will be used for small-group time, when work time will end, or how to maintain a safe classroom environment) creates a collaborative community of learners.

Here I engage in exploratory play with several children during outside time.

Praise versus encouragement

In the beginning, the concept of cutting out praise was completely new to me. Now, however, using acknowledgement and encouragement with children instead makes complete sense. This is because I understand that when I converse with children about their choices, accomplishments, or something they're excited about, I know that I am supporting their own personal growth. I am guiding children as they make personal connections to their work or other choices and decide things for themselves. I'm finally seeing how this relates to children's self-reflection. That is, when children are acknowledged and encouraged, they engage in a rich discourse about how they feel about and perceive what they have done. Praise, however, cuts off any conversation that may otherwise follow. When you tell a child "Good job," it pretty much closes the door to further discussion. Encouragement, on the other hand, opens up a conversation about the child's choices and keeps the excitement alive. Children spend

By scaffolding through conversation and shared ideas, I support children as they solve a problem with materials during snacktime.

more time engaged in a shared dialogue in which they explain things as well as think about (reflect on) their thought processes and experiences.

Planning and recall

When I began this journey, I'd never used the plan-do-review sequence before. This sequence is such an integral part of the HighScope Curriculum because it takes the intentionality with which we approach teaching (mindfully planning how we will support children) and puts it in the hands of children as they prepare for their day and make choices — through which they will actively engage in learning. As children plan and recall, they are growing as critical thinkers. The plan-do-review process also gives children the opportunity to stop and think when they change their minds about what they want to do, before they begin something new. Also, children may plan together, and the plan-do-review process gives them opportunities to problem solve and discuss their ideas, so they can experience a successful work time.

I've also gained an appreciation for how planning and recall allow for self-expression and language use. When children recall, they are often not only recalling about themselves, but are working together to remember what they may have done together. They use words to describe what they have done, as well as illustrations, symbols, gestures, and movements.

Large-group time

I have learned to weave into large-group time many opportunities for children to make choices. I have found that this is key to understanding and planning for this part of the daily routine. When the children are given choices — about how to move their bodies or the materials, about which body parts or materials to use, about how to express themselves while listening to music, and so on — they not only take responsibility for what happens and feel a sense of control but they also think critically as they make choices. All of these things help deepen children's interest in the activity and materials.

I have also come to understand that there are different types of movement. That is, not only is large-group time an opportunity for children to explore gross-motor movement and develop their large muscles but it is also an opportunity for *expression* through movement — that is, to use movement

I watch as a child makes a plan with metal lids that are labeled with the classroom areas and a magnet "fishing pole." After the child chooses her area, I listen as she tells me who she will play with and what materials she plans to use.

as a form of creative representation. Although I knew both types of movement were possible, I really didn't think about how various large-group time experiences could enhance both types of movement.

Small-group time

During my time at the Demonstration Preschool, I discovered how small-group times can incorporate many different skills, KDIs, and materials. These experiences can be planned based on the children's interests and/or the curriculum. There are so many opportunities to meet children at their developmental level and to support children as they engage with materials, language, curriculum content, adults, and one another. I now have the confidence I need to plan activities and to scaffold them based on children's individual needs and interests. I'm excited to be able to emphasize just how simple the ideas for small-group

I explore stretching movements with the children during large-group time.

times can be! Sometimes only one type of material is all that is needed (plus a simple backup material). Sometimes the children themselves can come up with an idea for small-group time. On other days, small-group time provides a wonderful opportunity for teachers to introduce brand-new materials. Regardless of your approach to finding ideas for varied small-group times, the children will always surprise you with a new way to use or blend materials. Their perspectives, as shared with one another through actions and conversation, mutually enhance the entire group's learning.

Daily planning

I had never practiced daily planning in the elementary and preschool programs in which I had taught before coming to the Demonstration Preschool. Instead, I planned weekly. Looking back, I realize that, while on the one hand it felt easier to have the whole week planned out in front of me, there were always modifications I needed to make. What I have learned is that planning

During small-group time, after watching a child create a pattern with his caps and discussing the process, I look for caps so that I can try out his ideas.

Teachers plan daily in the HighScope Demonstration Preschool classroom. They meet at the end of each day to discuss highlights of the day, problem-solve, talk about children's development, and make the next day's plan.

daily helps teachers accommodate children's changes in focus and interest. For us as teachers, it also brings intentionality back to the forefront each and every day — never to be out of focus.

Scaffolding

Schools often talk about *differentiation,* a term that refers to the modifications teachers make to meet the wide array of needs of *all* children in a classroom. It is more than just an educational buzz word; it has grown to be an important expectation and requirement of teachers. As intentional teachers in an active-learning classroom, we know that this means we must meet each child at his or her developmental level.

During our daily planning session, Shannon and I look for ways to scaffold (or differentiate) children's learning experiences so that all children's needs are met. We use several strategies to stay mindful of this and make this expectation visible throughout each part of our plan. First, we actually write down, on our daily planning sheet, our expectations for students who are at earlier, middle, and later levels of development, and this helps us see ways in which we can extend their development during the small-group-time part of the day. Then, in the classroom, we use acknowledgement and language-rich conversations to describe to the children exactly what is happening as we share experiences with one another. At the same time, we allow the children themselves to take planned experiences in new directions. For example, during small-group time, a teacher may have planned for children to build with blocks and compare heights of towers to be built, yet a child might be more interested in pretending that these blocks are cars of a train. In this instance, the teacher would scaffold by acknowledging the child's choice, trying similar ideas with his or her own set of blocks, and gently extending when appropriate (in this case, possibly by bringing in another aspect of comparison — perhaps by saying "I see that this train car is *longer/faster* than that train car" or by applying to the play scenario the child's new focus of pretend play: "I wonder *where* the trains are *going*.")

The COR and KDIs

In previous teaching experiences, I have had to fight for authentic assessments. What I love about the Child Observation Record (COR) is that the anecdotes provide authentic, concrete, and meaningful vignettes of how we observe children's language, connections, interactions, thought processes, and overall learning.

After starting to work at HighScope, somewhere along the line I began to see how the COR and KDIs complement one another. Sometimes I would reflect on the COR items when planning or thinking about the development of the children in my classroom, and sometimes I would refer to KDIs to do this. Eventually, I saw these sets come together, and I learned how to use both to support the children's engagement with curriculum content. (See Chapter 11, which starts on p. 169, for examples of this.)

Materials

The possibilities for materials in the preschool classroom are endless. I won't look at any "everyday" materials the same way ever again! I continue to make homemade play dough and bring in the dried sunflower heads that my grandparents save each year from their garden. But I also find myself asking if they happen to have an old TV or stereo remote that the kids can take apart, or what they plan on doing with all those extra scraps of wood in their home workshop. I save the plastic scoops from my boyfriend's chai tea containers to use in activities with kids. Once this year I spent over an hour collecting odd seed pods from a tree in my yard. I've also gone more "green" and saved cell phones, old scarves, calendars, and even a broken computer keyboard from the dumpster, for use in the classroom. A little creativity goes a long way, and if you have enough safe materials for a small group (and room to store them), the children in your classroom will have a great time and learn a lot while manipulating these odds and ends.

Additionally, I now place more value on high-quality, open-ended, natural materials (such as shells and rocks) that offer children choices for doing things on their own or collaboratively during work time. I've also begun thinking about classroom tools in a new light. Examples of tools we've used in the house area include ice cream scoops, whisks, and hand blenders. Tools we've used in the woodworking area include hammers, hand drills, and screwdrivers. Now I also think about how children will approach art, and I'd like to expose them to more professional artist's tools, in addition to all the various "odd" materials children can use to paint with.

Philosophy and adult-child interactions

Everything I do in teaching is an attempt to do what is in the best interests of children. I am always striving for excellence in education through developmentally appropriate practices. What I have loved about this journey is learning how to hone my teaching skills and really become more aware of the details of my practice. Creating a developmentally appropriate active-learning environment is all about intentionality — making meaningful connections between curriculum goals and children's needs and interests.

People always ask me what sets HighScope apart from other well-recognized early childhood programs. When I first started at HighScope, I used to answer that question by talking about the plan-do-review sequence. Sometimes I would also describe problem solving, and even praise versus encouragement. While these are very important pieces of the curriculum, I have recently come to realize that, to me, what sets HighScope apart is the strength and authenticity of trusting and engaging adult-child relationships. Now, the adult-child

A basket of shells in the toy area at the Demonstration Preschool.

interaction piece may seem very obvious, but it also takes a lot of thought and hard work to do well. Many teachers will tell you that they love working with children and that many children love and even adore their teachers. Children mean the world to me, and before teaching at HighScope, I had always had solid relationships with children. But what I learned most from HighScope is how to maintain notably strong adult-child relationships.

In a HighScope classroom, adults are actively engaging, interacting with, and sharing language with children. Teachers and children are *partners* in play throughout each and every part of the daily routine — that is, 100 percent of the time! There is a subtlety here that I didn't realize at first, and that is why it has taken a year's worth of reflection for me to fully answer this question about why I think HighScope is different. There is never a moment of the day, except perhaps during a medical emergency, that a teacher spends merely *managing* or *monitoring*. I think that sometimes in preschool, because the children are so young and "just playing," adults tend to think that they can step aside and merely monitor for a bit. Actually, I've noticed this also happens during elementary-school choice times or independent work times. I would attest that at least part of this has to do with the fact that play is not fully understood or valued. The power of play and the benefits for children's development — including social, emotional, analytical, creative, physical, mathematical, scientific, and language abilities — are highly underestimated by many. When teachers provide a thoughtfully created environment and a consistent daily routine, along with high-quality adult-child interactions, children are able to experience the world at their fingertips. With adults to support, guide, acknowledge, take cues from, listen to, and *learn from* them, children experience play on a whole new level.

I get down on this child's level to talk to her about her next plan during work time.

A Final Reflection

Teaching with the HighScope Curriculum has been a wonderful journey for me. Each step of the way, I have learned a great deal about education, myself, and my philosophies — on a number of levels. This book started with some basic journaling about small moments in the Demonstration Preschool. Although we had hoped this might become a book eventually, I also knew that writing down my experiences and reflections would make my own learning process stronger.

I have always had a specific interest in early childhood education. Even throughout my undergraduate studies, when I focused on the elementary level, my main interests were in kindergarten, and I knew that I would move on to study early childhood in graduate school. In addition, as I went on to work with children in grades 1 through 5, I was always mindful of developmentally appropriate practices, no matter the grade level.

I had never pictured myself teaching preschool — however, before teaching at HighScope, I had fallen into teaching two- and three-year-olds when I took an interim position before moving abroad to again teach elementary school. I hadn't thought I would enjoy my initial preschool teaching experience as much as I did.

When I returned from teaching in South America and began teaching at HighScope, I learned increasingly more about teaching preschoolers. Specifically, I came to understand a great deal about what truly are *best* practices in early childhood education. I have so appreciated gaining a better understanding of the whole range of child development.

As I've continued on in my professional career in education, I have come to realize an overwhelming and perplexing truth: *the more I know, the less I know.* What I mean by this is that the more I study and learn, the more I read and practice, the more I grow and change, the more I realize how much I still have to learn! Learning to teach at HighScope was a humbling experience, but I also know that I brought new perspectives and strengths to my position there as well.

Making a commitment to adopt a curriculum in its entirety in one's teaching, and really staying true to its key principles as well as its intricate details, can seem like an overwhelming undertaking. As one does this, it is important to seek out print and multimedia resources, support within the education community, and an attitude of patience with and positivity toward oneself. Though the journey may seem arduous at times, the benefits of such a process (in my case, the process of adopting HighScope's Curriculum in full) can have lasting effects on the children one nurtures each day, on their families, and on the educators and other professionals with whom one works.

Adopting a new curriculum is much like implementing the six steps to conflict resolution. When a conflict arises, in the moment it seems as though it would be so much faster and easier to just tell a child to stop a behavior and take turns, for example. But we all know that, in the long run, a much more constructive approach is for teachers and children to become strong problem solvers in the context of a supportive classroom community. In the same way, when teachers adopt new programs that work (and that are based on years of research and fundamental knowledge in the early childhood field), we can be tempted to take shortcuts and try only those elements of the program that come more easily to us. But the hard work it takes to study the program, start to implement it, and continue along the learning path pays off a great deal in the end. I know that my preschoolers at HighScope, my current students, and the students in my classrooms to come will all benefit from the challenging experiences I have had throughout this process. And I have the community of HighScope researchers, teachers, trainers, parents, and children to thank for that.

Afterword: Moving Ahead

I will take HighScope with me wherever I go.

I had planned on teaching and learning at HighScope for quite some time, and it has been difficult for me to leave HighScope and the Demonstration Preschool at the end of my first full year there. However, my personal life has taken me in a beautiful new direction, and I'm excited to bring my passion for teaching and my past experiences to bear in a new position as an early-elementary teacher.

I'm excited about adapting what I learned about the HighScope Curriculum for an early elementary setting. Active learning will remain ever-present in my classroom, as will having a consistent routine, a variety of materials, and supportive adult-child interactions. Where the lines blur a bit (and where I find myself back at the beginning again) is with classroom management and work time. In the end, I will need to find a way to do what is in the best interests of the children that I teach, while also adhering to building and district policies and philosophies. I know this will include finding creative ways to offer choices when and how I can, and using problem solving and natural consequences to teach responsibility and understanding. Teaching is always about balance; such challenges are similar to those I have faced before, and I will face them again. However, I now have a stronger understanding about how and why to advocate for the most developmentally appropriate practices. That's the point of all this. Reflection pairs nicely with intentionality. And although these two stir up challenging questions, both teachers and children reap rewards through this process of lifelong learning.

— Becky James

Appendix A: HighScope Preschool Curriculum Content

Key Developmental Indicators

A. Approaches to Learning

1. **Initiative:** Children demonstrate initiative as they explore their world.
2. **Planning:** Children make plans and follow through on their intentions.
3. **Engagement:** Children focus on activities that interest them.
4. **Problem solving:** Children solve problems encountered in play.
5. **Use of resources:** Children gather information and formulate ideas about their world.
6. **Reflection:** Children reflect on their experiences.

B. Social and Emotional Development

7. **Self-identity:** Children have a positive self-identity.
8. **Sense of competence:** Children feel they are competent.
9. **Emotions:** Children recognize, label, and regulate their feelings.
10. **Empathy:** Children demonstrate empathy toward others.
11. **Community:** Children participate in the community of the classroom.
12. **Building relationships:** Children build relationships with other children and adults.
13. **Cooperative play:** Children engage in cooperative play.
14. **Moral development:** Children develop an internal sense of right and wrong.
15. **Conflict resolution:** Children resolve social conflicts.

C. Physical Development and Health

16. **Gross-motor skills:** Children demonstrate strength, flexibility, balance, and timing in using their large muscles.
17. **Fine-motor skills:** Children demonstrate dexterity and hand-eye coordination in using their small muscles.
18. **Body awareness:** Children know about their bodies and how to navigate them in space.
19. **Personal care:** Children carry out personal care routines on their own.
20. **Healthy behavior:** Children engage in healthy practices.

D. Language, Literacy, and Communication[1]

21. **Comprehension**: Children understand language.

22. **Speaking**: Children express themselves using language.

23. **Vocabulary**: Children understand and use a variety of words and phrases.

24. **Phonological awareness**: Children identify distinct sounds in spoken language.

25. **Alphabetic knowledge**: Children identify letter names and their sounds.

26. **Reading**: Children read for pleasure and information.

27. **Concepts about print**: Children demonstrate knowledge about environmental print.

28. **Book knowledge**: Children demonstrate knowledge about books.

29. **Writing**: Children write for many different purposes.

30. **English language learning**: (If applicable) Children use English and their home language(s) (including sign language).

E. Mathematics

31. **Number words and symbols**: Children recognize and use number words and symbols.

32. **Counting**: Children count things.

33. **Part-whole relationships**: Children combine and separate quantities of objects.

34. **Shapes**: Children identify, name, and describe shapes.

35. **Spatial awareness**: Children recognize spatial relationships among people and objects.

36. **Measuring**: Children measure to describe, compare, and order things.

37. **Unit**: Children understand and use the concept of unit.

38. **Patterns**: Children identify, describe, copy, complete, and create patterns.

39. **Data analysis**: Children use information about quantity to draw conclusions, make decisions, and solve problems.

---

[1]Language, Literacy, and Communication KDIs 21–29 may be used for the child's home language(s) as well as English. KDI 30 refers specifically to English language learning.

F. Creative Arts

40. **Art**: Children express and represent what they observe, think, imagine, and feel through two- and three-dimensional art.

41. **Music**: Children express and represent what they observe, think, imagine, and feel through music.

42. **Movement**: Children express and represent what they observe, think, imagine, and feel through movement.

43. **Pretend play**: Children express and represent what they observe, think, imagine, and feel through pretend play.

44. **Appreciating the arts**: Children appreciate the creative arts.

G. Science and Technology

45. **Observing**: Children observe the materials and processes in their environment.

46. **Classifying**: Children classify materials, actions, people, and events.

47. **Experimenting**: Children experiment to test their ideas.

48. **Predicting**: Children predict what they expect will happen.

49. **Drawing conclusions**: Children draw conclusions based on their experiences and observations.

50. **Communicating ideas**: Children communicate their ideas about the characteristics of things and how they work.

51. **Natural and physical world**: Children gather knowledge about the natural and physical world.

52. **Tools and technology**: Children explore and use tools and technology.

H. Social Studies

53. **Diversity**: Children understand that people have diverse characteristics, interests, and abilities.

54. **Community roles**: Children recognize that people have different roles and functions in the community.

55. **Decision making**: Children participate in making classroom decisions.

56. **Geography**: Children recognize and interpret features and locations in their environment.

57. **History**: Children understand past, present, and future.

58. **Ecology**: Children understand the importance of taking care of their environment.

Appendix B: Additional Resources

Here are some resources that can help you on your HighScope learning journey. You can find out about these and much more at the HighScope website, www.highscope.org:

Books

- The HighScope Preschool Curriculum set:

    The HighScope Preschool Curriculum, by Ann S. Epstein and Mary Hohmann

    Approaches to Learning, by Ann S. Epstein

    Creative Arts, by Ann S. Epstein

    Language, Literacy, and Communication, by Ann S. Epstein

    Social and Emotional Development, by Ann S. Epstein

    Physical Development and Health, by Ann S. Epstein

    Mathematics, by Ann S. Epstein

    Science and Technology, by Ann S. Epstein

    Social Studies, by Ann S. Epstein

- *Lesson Plans for the First 30 Days: Getting Started With HighScope, Second Edition,* by Beth Marshall with Shannon Lockhart and Moya Fewson

- *Essentials of Active Learning in Preschool,* by Ann S. Epstein

- *You're Not My Friend Anymore! Illustrated Answers to Questions About Young Children's Challenging Behaviors,* by Betsy Evans

- *You Can't Come to My Birthday Party! Conflict Resolution With Young Children,* by Betsy Evans

- *I Belong: Active Learning for Children With Special Needs,* by Jan Dowling and Terri Mitchell

DVDs

- *Adult-Child Interaction*

- *The Daily Routine*

- *Plan-Do-Review in Action*

- *Large-Group Times for Active Learners*

- *Small-Group Times for Active Learners*

- *Outside Time for Active Learners*

- *The Indoor and Outdoor Learning Environment*

- *Supporting Children in Resolving Conflicts*

Assessment Tools

- Preschool Child Observation Record (COR)

- OnlineCOR

About the Author

Rebecca James was a preschool teacher and early childhood specialist at the HighScope Educational Research Foundation Demonstration Preschool throughout the time that this book was written. While at HighScope, Becky also worked on aligning state early learning standards with the Child Observation Record (COR), collected data for infant-toddler studies, presented at HighScope's international conference, wrote articles for HighScope's *ReSource* magazine and the online feature *Ideas from the Field* at HighScope's website, contributed to the development of the updated COR assessment, and became a certified HighScope teacher.

Becky is now a first grade teacher in the New York City Public Schools. She holds a bachelor of arts degree in elementary education from the University of Michigan and a masters degree in early childhood education from Eastern Michigan University. She has nearly eight years of experience in the field, working with toddler through fifth grade students in Michigan, New York, and abroad.